Dr. Seuss

The People to Know Series

Madeleine Albright
0-7660-1143-7

Neil Armstrong
0-89490-828-6

Isaac Asimov
0-7660-1031-7

Robert Ballard
0-7660-1147-X

Barbara Bush
0-89490-350-0

Willa Cather
0-89490-980-0

Bill Clinton
0-89490-437-X

Hillary Rodham Clinton
0-89490-583-X

Bill Cosby
0-89490-548-1

Walt Disney
0-89490-694-1

Bob Dole
0-89490-825-1

Marian Wright Edelman
0-89490-623-2

Bill Gates
0-89490-824-3

Ruth Bader Ginsberg
0-89490-621-6

John Glenn
0-7660-1532-7

Jane Goodall
0-89490-827-8

Al Gore
0-7660-1232-8

Tipper Gore
0-7660-1142-9

Billy Graham
0-7660-1533-5

Alex Haley
0-89490-573-2

Tom Hanks
0-7660-1436-3

Ernest Hemingway
0-89490-979-7

Ron Howard
0-89490-981-9

Steve Jobs
0-7660-1536-X

Helen Keller
0-7660-1530-0

John F. Kennedy
0-89490-693-3

Stephen King
0-7660-1233-6

John Lennon
0-89490-702-6

Maya Lin
0-89490-499-X

Jack London
0-7660-1144-5

Malcolm X
0-89490-435-3

Wilma Mankiller
0-89490-498-1

Branford Marsalis
0-89490-495-7

Anne McCaffrey
0-7660-1151-8

Barbara McClintock
0-89490-983-5

Rosie O'Donnell
0-7660-1148-8

Gary Paulsen
0-7660-1146-1

Christopher Reeve
0-7660-1149-6

Ann Richards
0-89490-497-3

Sally Ride
0-89490-829-4

Will Rogers
0-89490-695-X

Franklin D. Roosevelt
0-89490-696-8

Dr. Seuss
0-7660-2106-8

Steven Spielberg
0-89490-697-6

John Steinbeck
0-7660-1150-X

Martha Stewart
0-89490-984-3

Amy Tan
0-89490-699-2

Alice Walker
0-89490-620-8

Andy Warhol
0-7660-1531-9

Simon Wiesenthal
0-89490-830-8

Elie Wiesel
0-89490-428-0

Frank Lloyd Wright
0-7660-1032-5

People to Know

Dr. Seuss

Best-Loved Author

Carin T. Ford

Enslow Publishers, Inc.

40 Industrial Road   PO Box 38
Box 398   Aldershot
Berkeley Heights, NJ 07922   Hants GU12 6BP
USA   UK

http://www.enslow.com

Library of Congress Cataloging-in-Publication Data

Ford, Carin T.
   Dr. Seuss : best-loved author / Carin T. Ford.
      p. cm. — (People to know)
      Summary: A biography of the author of such books as "Green
Eggs and Ham" and "The Cat in the Hat."
   Includes bibliographical references and index.
   ISBN 0-7660-2106-8
    1. Seuss, Dr.—Juvenile literature. 2. Authors, American—20th century—
Biography—Juvenile literature. 3. Illustrators—United States—Biography—
Juvenile literature. 4. Children's literature—Authorship—Juvenile
literature. [1. Seuss, Dr. 2. Authors, American. 3. Illustrators.] I. Title.
II. Title: Doctor Seuss. III. Series.
   PS3513.E2Z674 2003
   813'.52—dc21
   [B]
                         2002010387

Printed in the United States of America

10 9 8 7 6 5 4 3 2 1

To Our Readers: We have done our best to make sure all Internet Addresses in this
book were active and appropriate when we went to press. However, the author and the
publisher have no control over and assume no liability for the material available on
those Internet sites or on other Web sites they may link to. Any comments or
suggestions can be sent by e-mail to comments@enslow.com or to the address on the
back cover.

Every effort has been made to locate all copyright holders of material used in this
book. If any errors or omissions have occurred, corrections will be made in future
editions of this book.

Illustration Credits: AP/Wide World Photos, pp. 6, 97, 98; Corbis Images,
pp. 61, 82; Corel Corporation, p. 35; Courtesy of the Ernest Hemingway
Collection, John Fitzgerald Kennedy Library, p. 38; Dartmouth College
Library, pp. 25, 30, 31, 65, 73, 77, 85, 89; Enslow Publishers Inc., pp. 9,
39; Hulton Archive, pp. 12, 44, 51; Library of Congress, pp. 16, 17; United
States Department of Defense, p. 20.

Cover Credits: AP/Wide World Photos

Contents

Dr. Seuss

Lucky Man

It all had to do with luck. According to Theodor Geisel—more commonly known as Dr. Seuss—he was a lucky man.

It was the late 1920s and Geisel was drawing cartoons for *Judge* magazine. He had been thrilled to be offered the job of cartoonist at a salary of seventy-five dollars a week. *Judge* was a popular weekly magazine with sales even higher than those of its closest competitor, *Life* magazine.

Geisel's cartoons for *Judge* contained many of the strange and wonderful creatures that would appear in his books in years to come. One of his magazine covers contained an illustration of an elephant who very much resembled Horton from *Horton Hatches the Egg* and *Horton Hears a Who*. Other beasts looked like Yooks, Bar-ba-loots, and Loraxes.

Geisel's lucky streak began when he drew a cartoon set in a medieval castle. It showed a fierce dragon standing threateningly over a knight in armor, who was lying in bed. In the caption, the knight said, "Darn it all, another Dragon. And just after I'd sprayed the whole castle with Flit!"[1]

Flit was one of two commonly used insecticides at the time. The other was Fly Tox.

"I didn't know which one to use in the cartoon," Geisel said, "so I tossed a coin and it came up heads, for Flit."[2]

Geisel was lucky. He'd made the right choice.

Grace Cleaves, the wife of an advertising executive for Flit, was flipping through *Judge* magazine at the hairdresser's one day when she saw the cartoon. Cleaves begged her husband to hire Geisel to draw Flit's advertisements.

Geisel was luckier than he knew. The hairdresser Cleaves usually went to did not have *Judge* in its salon. But Cleaves was at a different salon because her hairdresser did not have any openings that particular day. And that was where she happened to see the magazine.

Geisel was hired. He drew advertisements for Flit for more than fifteen years. Just like his cartoons, many of his Flit ads resembled the artwork that would appear in his future children's books. So did the text. One advertisement read:

> If Flit can knock *this* monster stiff,
> mere bugs and stuff won't last *one whiff!*[3]

The Flit ads were very popular. They usually

Seuss's cartoons made ads for Flit insecticide popular in the late 1920s.

showed a number of people who were in immediate danger of being attacked by oversized Seuss-like insects. The people would cry, "Quick, Henry, the Flit!"

The phrase, "Quick, Henry, the Flit!" began to be heard in everyday conversations. Comedians would use the line as part of their acts. Even a song was based on the phrase. Sales of the bug spray increased and Geisel's drawings appeared in newspapers and on billboards.

Geisel was acquiring a reputation, if not fame. He was also earning good money. Because he did not have a routine work schedule, he was able to spend time traveling. Geisel journeyed all around the world with his wife Helen.

In the summer of 1936, Geisel and his wife were sailing home from Europe on the M.S. *Kungsholm.* The ship was in the middle of the Atlantic Ocean when a storm sprang up. It was too rough to go out on deck, so Geisel headed down to the bar to wait out the bad weather. The steady rhythm of the ship's motors seemed to pound in his head.

"To keep from going nuts, I began reciting silly words to the rhythm of the engines," Geisel said.

He took out some sheets of the ship's stationery. As the motors continued their rhythm, Geisel began to write:

A stupid horse and wagon . . . horse and chariot . . . chariot pulled by flying cat . . . flying cat pulling at Viking ship . . . Viking ship sailing up a volcano . . . (use all).

"These are the first words I ever wrote in the field of writing for children," Geisel said many years later.[4]

Turning these words into a book was no easy task for Geisel. Over a period of six months, he wrote and rewrote the story. Geisel admitted he did not know anything about children's books. But he said that he wanted to make sure it was the kind of story that would inspire children to "turn page after page."[5] He worked painstakingly on the drawings, the text, and the humor.

"The problem with writing a book in verse," Geisel said, "is to be successful it has to sound like you knocked it off on a rainy Friday afternoon. It has to sound easy."[6]

Geisel was always a perfectionist, and the process of writing would never be easy for him.

But he thought this story was good.

It revolves around a boy named Marco who wants to have something interesting to tell his father about his walk home from school. But the walk is boring, so Marco begins creating some amazing sights and events that happen along the way. Throughout the story, Marco's imagination takes a continually wilder turn.

Titling the book, *A Story That No One Can Beat*, Geisel decided it was time to get it published.

Unfortunately, the publishing world did not agree.

Twenty-nine publishers rejected the manuscript. They did not want to take the risk of publishing a book that was so different from all the other children's books in the libraries and bookstores. Fantasy and rhyme was not a combination the publishers believed would sell well. They also tended to prefer books that delivered moral messages to children. Geisel's story was not about morals. It was about *fun*.

Geisel was discouraged by the rejections. Should he give up the idea of getting his book published?

But again, he got lucky.

Geisel was walking down Madison Avenue in New York City with the manuscript under his arm one day.

Seuss attributed his success mostly to luck although he worked for hours on each sentence and each sketch.

He bumped into an old college friend, Mike McClintock, who asked him what he was carrying.

"A book that no one will publish," said Geisel. "I'm lugging it home to burn."[7]

McClintock suggested that Geisel come to his office right away. Only hours earlier, McClintock had been made an editor of children's books at Vanguard Press.

McClintock liked the story. So did Vanguard's president, James Henle. But both men had a problem with the book—the title.

Renamed *And to Think That I Saw It on Mulberry Street*, the book was published in 1937. Geisel also named the young boy featured in the book Marco, after McClintock's son.

And to Think That I Saw It on Mulberry Street received good reviews from the start. Geisel had stepped into the world of children's literature, and he would never turn back. Over the next fifty-four years, he would turn out forty-six more books.

Years later, Geisel remembered how close he'd come to burning that manuscript. If he'd been walking along the other side of Madison Avenue, he might never have become a children's book author.

"See," he said, "everything has to do with luck."[8]

Early Years

Theodor Seuss Geisel was born March 2, 1904, in Springfield, Massachusetts. Nicknamed Ted, he was Theodor and Henrietta Geisel's only son. His sister, Margaretha—called Marnie—was two years older. Later, in 1906, the Geisels had another child, Henrietta, who died of pneumonia before she was two years old.

Springfield was located about one hundred miles (160 kilometers) west of Boston and had a large German population. Ted's paternal grandfather, Theodor Geisel, had sailed to America from Germany in the 1860s. In America, Theodor Geisel ran a brewery, where alcoholic beverages are produced. It was called Kalmbach and Geisel, but was jokingly referred to as "Come Back and Guzzle" by the residents of Springfield.

Ted's grandfather on his mother's side was George J. Seuss—pronounced "Zoice" in German. Seuss and his wife had immigrated to America from southern Germany. They ran a bakery in Springfield, and Ted's mother worked there. Henrietta Seuss was not able to attend college, as she had hoped, because she was needed in the bakery.

But Henrietta was a determined woman. Six feet tall and about two hundred pounds, she was strong, pretty, and an accomplished high diver. Since she had been denied the chance of receiving a college education, Henrietta resolved to do the next best thing: She would make sure her children attended college.

She read constantly to Ted and Marnie. Often at bedtime, the children fell asleep to the soft, rhythmic sound of their mother's voice.

Ted commented years later that it was these bedtime stories that most influenced the rhythms he used in his writing.

If Ted's mother influenced the rhythms of his verses, it was his father who encouraged him to strive for perfection in everything he did.

Mr. Geisel had been an expert marksman when he was younger. At one time, he held the world record for shooting at two hundred yards (183 kilometers). He had a target from one of his competitions with holes piercing the bull's-eye. Ted framed it and kept it near him all his life.

"That target reminds me to reach for excellence," Ted explained.[1]

Mr. Geisel helped manage the brewery. He was also a member of the parks board of Springfield.

Ted was born in Springfield, Massachusetts, in 1904.

Forest Park, which was near Ted's house, was extremely large with hills and ponds. Best of all, there was a zoo in the park. Ted enjoyed going to the Springfield Zoo with his father. He usually brought his sketchpad along with him. These early drawings hinted at the Seuss-like animals that would one day appear in his books. Ted liked taking the features of one animal and drawing them onto another. In his sketches, tigers often had wings, and giraffes frequently appeared with elephant ears.

"I've loved animals for as long as I can remember," Ted said. "It's a wonder that after all the animals I've seen, I can't make them true to life. When I do an elephant the poor beast usually winds up not only with too many joints in his legs but with too many legs."[2]

Ted looked up to his father. Years later, he would dedicate one of his books, *If I Ran the Circus*, to him: "This book is for my dad, Big Ted of Springfield, the finest man I'll ever know."[3]

Ted seemed to be as interested in observing animals as in drawing them. On the night of April 20, 1910, his father took him out to a field so they could watch Halley's Comet shoot across the sky. Ted remembered that night. But he recalled being even more impressed when, for the very first time, he saw an owl sitting in an elm tree.

Ted made sure he always had pencils and crayons

Forest Park was home to the Springfield Zoo that Ted liked to visit with his father.

with him. Sometimes he would climb up to the attic in his house and draw animals on the walls there. His mother did not scold him. Instead, she consistently praised and encouraged Ted and his work.

"Everything you do is great," she would say, "just go ahead and do it."[4]

And he did. Once he showed his mother a drawing he had made of an animal at the zoo. The creature had enormous ears hanging way below its feet. When Ted told his mother the animal was called a "Wynnmph," his mother said of course it was and it was absolutely wonderful![5]

Ted's interest in drawing was equal to his interest in reading. Perhaps his favorite book as a young boy was *The Hole Book* by Peter Newell. It told the story of a bullet that flew crazily throughout a house, making holes everywhere. There was a hole in every page of the book, as the bullet made its wild way about the house. What finally stopped the path of the bullet was a very hard cake.

Ted enjoyed reading so much that his mother would use books to bribe him. She signed Ted up for piano lessons and when he did well on the instrument, she took her son to the bookstore across the street and bought him the book of his choice. Ted especially liked a series of books called *The Rover Boys*. This collection of books was written by Edward Stratemeyer, under the name Arthur M. Winfield. Billed as "The Rover Boys Series for Young Americans," the books told of the adventures of three boys named Tom, Dick, and Sam. Some of the titles in the series were, *The Rover Boys at School, The*

Rover Boys on the Great Lakes, and *The Rover Boys in the Mountains*. A second series of Rover Boys books featured the sons of Tom, Dick, and Sam.

When Ted was twelve, he entered a contest sponsored by the local newspaper's advertising department. He submitted a cartoon of a fisherman reeling in a very large fish. Ted won first place.

He also enjoyed playing the banjo, the mandolin, and acting in school plays. For the most part, Ted's childhood was a happy one. But there was one painful incident that occurred when he was fourteen. It would haunt him forever.

The year was 1918, and the United States was fighting in World War I. One of the countries the United States was fighting was Germany. Many Americans felt hostile toward people who came from German backgrounds. Ted and Marnie were extremely sensitive about their heritage. Sometimes they were jeered on the playground and as they walked home from school.

Ted was a member of the Boy Scouts and took part in a fund-raiser that involved selling war bonds, a kind of savings bond that helped the United States government finance the war. He was glad to have the chance of proving how patriotic he was. When Ted learned he was one of the top-ten sellers of war bonds among the Springfield Boy Scouts, he was very proud. The ten boys were to receive special medals for their work from former president Theodore Roosevelt. Thousands of people—including Ted's family and relatives—filled the town's auditorium to watch the

Boy Scouts sold bonds to help the war effort during World War I. This World War I poster encourages support for the Boy Scouts' bond sales.

ceremony. Standing at the end of the line, Ted waited with excitement to receive his medal.

Nine boys accepted their medals, saluted the former president, and walked off the stage. Soon, only Ted was left.

But there were no more medals. Roosevelt had run out.

With a frown, Roosevelt looked down at Ted and loudly asked the boy what he was doing there. Feeling totally humiliated, Ted hurried off the stage. From that day on, Ted was afraid to appear in public. Even after he had become famous as Dr. Seuss, Ted made excuses whenever possible to avoid speaking in public.

When Ted entered Central High School, he was a tall, dark-haired, slightly awkward teenager. It was while Ted was in high school that his father was made the head of the brewery company, Kalmbach and Geisel. But the day Mr. Geisel took charge of the company, a Prohibition law was passed making the sale and manufacture of alcoholic beverages illegal. Because of Prohibition, Mr. Geisel was left without a job. Eventually, his voluntary position with the parks board turned into the paying position of park superintendent.

While he was in high school, Ted took part in a variety of school activities. He enjoyed playing the mandolin—a pear-shaped musical instrument with four to six strings—and formed a mandolin club. He also appeared in several school productions, including Shakespeare's *Twelfth Night*, and was secretary in the student government.

Ted was a good student, although not a top one like his sister. He did not work very hard and was happy getting B's without putting forth much effort. English was his favorite subject; he disliked math and Latin. Sometimes, he skipped Latin class and went to the movies instead.

Yet when Ted was older, he said studying Latin actually had a large influence on his writing. He said Latin gave him a love and respect for language.

"It allows you to adore words—take them apart and find out where they come from," he said.[6]

In spite of his interest in drawing, Ted only attended one art class in his life. It was not a good experience.

While working on a picture, Ted turned his painting upside down and continued working on it from that perspective. The art teacher told Ted that a true artist would never turn his painting upside down.

"That teacher wanted me to draw the world as it is," Ted said. "I wanted to draw things as I saw them."[7]

The teacher told Ted he did not have any artistic talent.

"It's the only reason I went on—to prove that teacher wrong," Ted said.[8]

Ted was able to combine his interest in writing and drawing on the school newspaper, *The Recorder*. He drew cartoons and soon was also writing jokes and poems. Occasionally, he wrote under a different name. Sometimes, he called himself Pete the Pessimist. Other times, he was T. S. LeSieg, "Geisel" spelled backwards. Years later, Ted would use this name on some of his books.

The only area where Ted never seemed to show any interest was athletics. Mr. Geisel hoped to change this by having his son take fencing lessons. Along with fencing, Ted worked with his coach on rope climbing and vaulting. But he never enjoyed sports. He wound up managing his high-school soccer team rather than playing on it. Unfortunately, the team lost every game. When Ted's father gave him his own canoe, Ted would only use it occasionally when he paddled with his school friends.

As his high-school graduation drew near, Ted needed to decide where he would attend college. He had particularly liked a young English teacher named Edwin A. ("Red") Smith. Smith was in his early twenties and had recently graduated from Dartmouth College in Hanover, New Hampshire. He made his English classes fun and interesting. He introduced Ted to the writings of Hilaire Belloc. Ted later said he was strongly influenced by the rhymes and rhythms of Belloc's poems.

Ted decided to attend the same college as Red Smith. He applied for admission to Dartmouth College.

3

Starting to Write

Ted traveled to Dartmouth College in September 1921. The school was four hours by train from Ted's home in Springfield.

Money for the Geisel family was tight since Ted's father was still unemployed at this time. Two years earlier, Ted's Grandfather Geisel had died and left an inheritance. The tuition money—two hundred fifty dollars a year—came out of this inheritance.

At the time that Ted entered Dartmouth, the college was interested in enrolling students from a variety of different backgrounds, and not just those who came from wealthy families. Ted certainly did not have wealth. He was also the first Geisel to attend college in the United States. Neither his father nor his grandfather had a college degree. His high school had not been prestigious, since it was public rather than private.

Influenced by Red Smith, Ted decided to major in English. Quickly, he became involved with the college's newspaper as well as its humor magazine, *Jack-O-Lantern*. He created cartoons for the

Sketching interested Geisel more than his classes when he entered Dartmouth College. This yearbook photo is dated 1925.

magazine, which allowed him to combine his love of drawing and writing.

Although fraternities were a big part of life at Dartmouth, Ted was not involved in them during his freshman year. College fraternities are organizations of male students (sororities are for women). Fraternity names are made up of Greek letters and usually the group has various secret rituals that are only known to members.

Students cannot join whichever fraternity they are interested in. They must be invited by current members. Students are chosen for the different fraternities during Pledge Week. To "pledge" a fraternity, means to promise to join.

Ted did not show any interest in joining a fraternity during Pledge Week, nor did he receive any invitations. Instead, he spent a lot of time at the *Jacko* office, often until late at night. He was looking ahead to the future, hoping to one day become the magazine's editor. Once, some staff members arrived at the magazine office after breakfast and found Ted sound asleep with his head on his typewriter.

Ted tended to be quiet during his first year at college, but he was always cheerful. He was funny in a good-natured way and according to some of his friends, he liked to laugh.

Because Ted seemed to be spending so much time working on the humor magazine, his studies suffered. Ted's grade point average that first semester hovered around a C.

Mr. Geisel was not happy about his son's grades. Yet both parents considered Ted to be unique and creative. They did not want to see him lose those qualities. But Ted's father did urge his son to try to get more out of college academically.

During Ted's summer at home in Springfield after freshman year, he worked at various jobs. But his most enjoyable hours were spent sketching.

The following year, Ted's schedule was filled with German and English literature, economics, zoology, and botany. Ted's sketchbook accompanied him to all these classes. As usual, animals figured strongly in his doodles. One of Ted's classmates owned a beagle dog named Spot. Ted sketched the beagle wearing a pair of antlers. Max, the dog in *How the Grinch Stole Christmas!*, may have been based on this early drawing of Spot.

Ted also helped take care of two bear cubs named Whiskey and Soda. The cubs belonged to Pete Blodgett, a classmate of Ted's. Blodgett knew the hunter who had shot the cubs' mother, and he wanted to make sure the cubs were cared for. The animals were kept in a wooded area that had been fenced off. The cubs stayed at Dartmouth through the winter— when they were hibernating—but Blodgett needed to find a home for them when spring came. They were climbing trees and interfering with traffic. A zoo in Ohio agreed to take the cubs, so Ted and Blodgett put the animals into a barred cage and sent them off on the train.

Ted managed the school's soccer team and played mandolin in the orchestra. But the majority of his time was spent working in the *Jacko* office. In 1923, he was elected to the magazine's art staff. By this time, Ted was known around campus because of his cartoons for *Jacko*.

During his second year at Dartmouth, Ted became a member of the Sigma Phi Epsilon fraternity. However, he was not interested in fraternity life and did not get very involved in its activities.

When Ted was a junior, he moved in with another student in order to save money. It did not matter to Ted that he had left his dormitory room. He assumed he would be spending most of his time at the *Jacko* office.

In his third year, Ted's grades began to show signs of improvement. He said he "discovered the excitement of 'marrying' words to pictures"[1] and especially enjoyed a creative writing course taught by W. Bensfield Pressey. The professor often invited students to his house, where he served cocoa and asked everyone to share the stories they had written. He was a kind man who encouraged students with their work, just as Red Smith had encouraged Ted in high school.

During one of these evenings, Ted bragged that he could write creatively on any subject. He decided to turn the railroad timetables for Boston and Maine into a humorous book review.

"Nobody in the class thought it was funny except Ben and me," Ted recalled.[2]

In some of Ted's classes, professors talked about trips they had made through Europe. This aroused in Ted a desire to travel that lasted for most of his life. During college, a catchphrase among students was, "Oh, the places you'll go! The people you'll meet!"[3] Ted would remember this many years later when writing the title for one his books.

In 1924, when Ted was completing his junior year, he achieved a goal he had set for himself at the start of college. He became editor-in-chief of *Jacko*. It seemed clear at this point that he was headed for a career in writing.

Ted signed up for several English courses during his final year at Dartmouth, including writing, poetry, and literature. He was enjoying his senior year. He liked editing *Jacko*, was interested in his classes, and led an active social life on campus. But that spring, Ted wound up in trouble.

Prohibition was still in effect, making it illegal to drink an alcoholic beverage. Yet Ted and several of his friends were drinking gin one night and were getting increasingly noisy. Ted was living in an apartment at the time, and his landlord made a phone call to the local police, who raided the gathering.

The school administration put the young men on probation because they had broken the law. Not only did Ted have to write a letter to his parents informing them of what had happened, he was not allowed to continue as editor-in-chief of *Jacko*.

Ted had to abide by the school's decision. Yet he was determined to continue writing and drawing. Since his name could not appear in the magazine, he made numerous submissions that did not contain a signature. For some of his sketches and cartoons, though, he made up pseudonyms: L. Burbank, Thos. Mottsborne, and D.G. Rossetti. Another pseudonym was his middle name, Seuss.

Geisel enjoyed editing the Jack-O-Lantern magazine at Dartmouth College.

". . . That's how 'Seuss' first came to be used as my signature," he said, "the 'Dr.' was added later on."[4]

As the time for graduation approached, Ted applied for a fellowship to attend Oxford University in England. The scholarship would provide the money for Ted to receive an advanced degree in English literature at the prestigious English college.

When Ted's father learned of his son's plans, he became excited. Not only did he tell his friends that Ted would be attending Oxford, he also informed Maurice Sherman, the editor of the local newspaper in Springfield. Ted's picture, along with the story of his plans, ran the next day in the paper. Many of

Geisel was voted "Least Likely to Succeed" by his fraternity brothers at Dartmouth. Pictured here is Dartmouth Hall.

Mr. Geisel's acquaintances congratulated him on the exciting news.

Unfortunately, Ted did not win the fellowship. But Mr. Geisel felt it would look foolish if his son did not travel to England since the story had already been published in the paper. He decided to pay for Ted's Oxford education himself.

Ted had enjoyed his four years at Dartmouth. He finished his academic career there with a C average. Although Ted had been voted "Class Artist" and "Class Wit" in high school, his fraternity brothers voted him, "Least Likely to Succeed" at Dartmouth.

On June 23, 1925, Ted graduated from college. After a summer of writing humorous verses for his hometown newspaper, Ted left for England.

European Travels

Ted Geisel was twenty-one when he began attending Lincoln College, a part of Oxford University. It was a cold fall day when he arrived. He had on a tweed jacket and a woolen scarf. Under his arm, he carried the typewriter he had used at Dartmouth College. He had hopes of eventually becoming a college professor.

Oxford University has a long and lively history. It is the oldest English-speaking university in the world. Although the date it was originally founded is unclear, teaching did take place at Oxford as early as 1096. By the thirteenth century, buildings were established so students could live at the university. And by the fourteenth century, the university was known and respected as a place of learning.

Some famous graduates of Oxford include: explorer Sir Walter Raleigh (1572), philosopher Thomas Hobbes (1608), founder of Pennsylvania William Penn (1660), author Oscar Wilde (1874), soldier and statesman "Lawrence of Arabia" (1907), author J. R. R. Tolkien (1911), and poet T. S. Eliot (1914).

Although Geisel was attending a highly prestigious university, he quickly found that the courses he was taking in English literature did not interest him. He studied the works of such great English writers as Geoffrey Chaucer, John Milton, and John Keats. In one class, the professor spent two hours discussing William Shakespeare's use of periods, commas, and semicolons in his play *King Lear*.

Geisel was bored. He also felt like an outsider. World War I had ended only seven years earlier, and Geisel was self-conscious about his German heritage. Called the Great War at the time, World War I lasted from 1914 to 1918. The United States was allied with Great Britain, France, Russia, and Japan. Fighting against these Allied Powers were the empires of Germany and Austria-Hungary. Nearly 10 million people lost their lives in the war.

Another problem for Geisel was that he did not feel as smart as the other students. Although he went through the usual daily routine of attending chapel in the morning, followed by lectures and classes, he did not consider himself a deep thinker. To Geisel, it seemed as if he was the only one who was not interested in his classes.

Geisel did make some friends, however. Joseph Sagmaster was from Cincinnati and like Geisel, was

Despite Oxford University's prestige, Geisel was bored there.

interested in writing. Fred Stokvis from Holland and a young woman named Mirable, who was related to the Earl of Devonshire, also befriended Geisel.

In class, his mind wandered, and he spent much of his time doodling in his black notebook with metal rings. Soon, there were more drawings than notes on the lectures. On the unlined paper, Geisel sketched knights in armor, students in his literature class, daggers, and of course, his animals.

The animals were cartoonlike, with a large number of what Geisel labelled "flying cows and strange beasts." By the last page of the notebook, "there are no notes on English literature at all. There are just strange beasts," Geisel later recalled.[1]

It was obvious to everyone—including Geisel's professors—that Oxford University was not the place for him. It was particularly clear to a small young woman from New Jersey named Helen Palmer. Five years older than Geisel, Palmer sat next to him and watched with interest as he sketched in his notebook.

She admired his drawing of a flying cow one day and told him, "You're crazy to be a professor. What you really want to do is draw."[2]

According to Geisel's friend Sagmaster, it was a case of love at first sight. The couple was formally introduced at a social gathering. They ignored everyone in the room except for each other and quickly began spending a lot of their time together.

Helen had a vivacious personality, but she had never been very healthy. She had suffered from polio as a child. There were no vaccines at that time for this infectious disease, which had been around since ancient times. (A vaccine was finally developed in 1952). Polio can permanently cause some of the body's muscles to waste away. As a result, Helen was left with a slightly off-balance smile.

She had graduated from Wellesley College in 1920 and had always hoped to attend Oxford. When she arrived there, it had only been four years since the university opened its doors to women.

Ted and Helen went their separate ways during Christmas vacation. Helen traveled back to the United States, while Geisel toured France with Sagmaster and some other friends.

When school resumed, Geisel and Helen purchased a motorcycle so they could travel around more easily. But there was a university rule that said first-year students were not allowed to own motor vehicles.

Geisel, however, figured out a way to avoid getting into trouble. He bought dead ducks that had been plucked of their feathers and tied them to the front of the motorcycle. This way, he looked like a delivery boy for a poultry shop. During one of these rides, Geisel took too wide a turn, landing himself and Helen in a ditch. Geisel said that was when he and Helen became engaged.

Although the couple enjoyed traveling around the countryside, Geisel knew Oxford was not for him. He called his studies "astonishingly irrelevant."[3] He also realized he was not meant to be a college professor.

In 1926, one of Geisel's teachers advised him to journey through Europe. He should go to the museums there and learn about history, the teacher said.

Geisel did travel to France with Helen during Easter vacation. They met up with Helen's mother in Paris and told her that they "seemed to be engaged."[4]

When the couple returned to Oxford after their four-week break, Geisel spent very little time on schoolwork. He had decided to follow his professor's advice and leave college in order to tour Europe. Helen planned to continue her education at Oxford, working toward a master's degree.

In June, Geisel's parents and sister journeyed to England. They were pleased to meet Helen before continuing their travels through France, Germany, and Switzerland. Together, they visited many relatives—both Geisels and Seusses—who lived in Europe.

Once his family had left, Geisel continued his travels. He wandered happily around Paris and stayed as far away from tourists as he possibly could. Paris at that time had attracted numerous writers such as Theodore Dreiser, author of *An American Tragedy,* and Ernest Hemingway, whose novels included *The Sun Also Rises.*

Geisel recalled seeing Hemingway, twenty-seven, smoking a pipe and writing on a pad of paper:

"What he was writing I never knew," said Geisel. "I was scared . . . to walk over and ask him, lest he ask me what I was writing. I was a twenty-two-year-old kid writing knock-kneed limericks about goats and cheese and other stuff that I couldn't sell. He was probably writing *A Farewell to Arms.*"[5]

For a short time, Geisel registered at the Sorbonne, a university in Paris, France. One of his

teachers had suggested that Geisel work on an assignment about writer Jonathan Swift. Geisel was supposed to find out whether Swift had written anything between the ages of sixteen and seventeen. The project would take him about two years. If it turned out Swift had not written anything during that time, Geisel would get neither a degree nor any

Geisel was afraid to approach renowned author Ernest Hemingway when he ran into him in Paris.

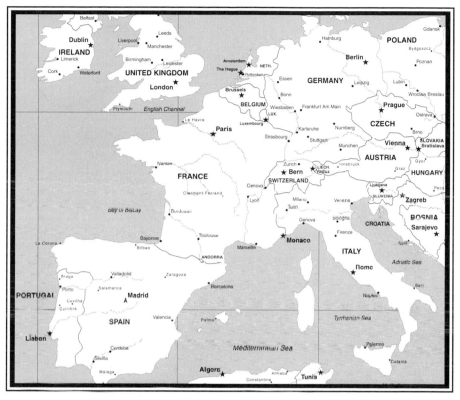

After leaving Oxford, Geisel toured Europe to study history, literature, and art.

credit for doing the assignment. Not surprisingly, he decided against doing the work.

Determined to put academic life behind him, Geisel recalled immediately "booking myself on a cattle boat to Corsica."[6] In Italy, Geisel jokingly said he concentrated on painting "donkeys for about a month."[7]

Closer to the truth is that Geisel traveled through Italy. He spent time with Helen, who was there with her mother. He also visited museums in the city of

Florence. He made numerous drawings as he wandered about. He sketched a cartoonlike version of Romulus and Remus, two brothers in Roman mythology. And he drew a tusked dragon with a long, swirling tail. The dragon was taken from Piero di Cosimo's painting entitled *Perseus Frees Andromeda,* which hung in Florence's Uffizi Gallery. Never again did Geisel turn to art history for his own sketches.

By this time, Helen had finished her work at Oxford and eventually returned to the United States, hoping to find a teaching job. Geisel moved on to Rome, where he continued sketching. He also wrote a novel, which he never sold. Geisel claimed he wrote part of the novel in Italian because he was influenced by a writer, Carl Van Vechten, who did the same in his book.

"I lapsed into Italian . . . for pages at a time," said Geisel. "I don't even speak Italian. I picked up the manuscript a few years ago—it was very long and mercifully never published—and couldn't understand a word of it."[8]

Geisel said he "eventually boiled the whole book down to a two-line joke and sold it to a magazine."[9]

In February 1927, Geisel sailed for New York. His future was uncertain, but he knew he was through attending school. He also knew he was going to marry Helen.

Taking Off

Geisel and Helen were engaged, but Geisel would not consider marriage until he was earning a steady income. When he returned to the United States, he visited Helen briefly in New York City and then rode the train to Springfield, Massachusetts.

Using his father's desk, Geisel worked on jokes and cartoons and mailed them off to a number of magazines. His curious animals continued to make their way into his sketches—such as the Hippocrass, a two-legged animal with wings and horns.

In the spring, Geisel traveled to New York with his portfolio visiting publishing houses, advertising agencies, and film companies in hopes of being hired as a staff writer or artist. He did not have much success. A few magazine editors expressed interest in his illustrations, but not enough to keep Geisel from being depressed when he returned to Springfield.

He did not give up, however. He sent out letters to several New York magazines, proposing a series of cartoons and poems. He waited. No one took him up on his offer.

Then finally, after several months, Geisel finally received the news he'd been hoping for. *The Saturday Evening Post* had purchased one of his cartoons and included a check for twenty-five dollars. The cartoon showed two American tourists who compare their trip to Lawrence of Arabia as they ride on camels.

The magazine published the cartoon on July 16, 1927. Geisel had signed his name "Seuss," although the magazine added Theodor Seuss Geisel.

Geisel was sure this sale would be the first of many. So he moved to New York City to begin his career as a cartoonist. Having little money, he shared an apartment in Greenwich Village with a friend from college. It was noisy and infested with rats. Before going to bed every night, Geisel and his roommate would stand on chairs and use canes to drive the rats out of the apartment.

Geisel quickly landed a job as a writer and artist for *Judge* magazine. Calling itself the "world's wittiest weekly," *Judge* paid Geisel a salary of seventy-five dollars a week.

Between Geisel's salary and the money Helen was earning from her teaching position at a private girls' school in Orange, New Jersey, the couple felt the time was right to get married. Their wedding was held on Nov. 29, 1927, four weeks after the original date had been set. Geisel's sister was due to give birth to her first child four weeks earlier, and no one wanted there to be a conflict between the two important events.

The wedding was a small gathering at Helen's home with about forty friends and members of Geisel's family. Breaking with the tradition of the time, Helen did not like the idea of being "given away." So instead of her brother leading her downstairs, Helen's mother walked with her into the living room, and the ceremony began.

Following the wedding, there was a brief reception and then a champagne supper in a nearby bar that sold alcohol (illegally) in spite of Prohibition. Then the couple traveled to Atlantic City, New Jersey, where they spent their honeymoon. Geisel was able to pay for his stay at the Hotel Traymore in exchange for advertising space in *Judge* magazine.

He began work at *Judge* in the third week of October in 1927. As part of the *Judge* staff, Geisel published his first cartoon, which showed two unicyclists conversing while they sat atop very tall unicycles. One commented to the other, "And to think that today I could have been the wife of a six-day bicycle racer, if I hadn't listened to your rot about Higher Art."[1] Geisel liked to play with words. Here he was toying with the *height* of the unicycle and *high* art.

Unfortunately, because of the magazine's financial problems, Geisel's paycheck dropped to fifty dollars a week a few weeks later. Shortly after that, *Judge* stopped paying its writers and illustrators altogether. Instead of money, employees would receive products from the magazine's advertisers. For example, Geisel

Geisel relied on his unusual animal drawings early into his career as a cartoonist.

was given one hundred cartons of shaving cream, nearly two thousand nail clippers, and numerous cases of soda.

The apartment where Geisel and Helen lived was not much better than the one Geisel had previously inhabited. Located on Eighteenth Street, the apartment stood across the street from a stable. It was a common occurrence for horses to die and simply be dragged into the street and left there. The odor was terrible. There was also a lot of crime in the neighborhood. Geisel always carried a cane with a switchblade in it in case he was assaulted.

Geisel created a cartoon series for *Judge* called "Boids and Beasties." Again, he relied on his unusual animal drawings. Some of these sketches came from the doodlings in his Oxford notebooks. He was now signing his name "Dr. Theophrastus Seuss" and before long, "Dr. Seuss." He might not have received a doctorate degree from Oxford, but he could still have a title, he decided. Other pseudonyms Geisel used early in his career were: Theo. Seuss 2nd, Dr. Theophilus Seuss, Ph. D., I.Q., H2SO4.[2] He said he was saving the name "Geisel" for the day he wrote his novel.

During the course of his career at *Judge*, Theodore Roosevelt, Jr. sent a letter to the magazine, asking for an original drawing by Dr. Seuss. Interestingly, Roosevelt's father was the former president who had frightened Geisel as a boy when he was not given a medal for selling war bonds as a Boy Scout.

Geisel's career took off when *Judge* published a cartoon he had drawn picturing a knight lying in bed with a fierce dragon hovering over him.

The cartoon made use of Flit insecticide, and Geisel was hired immediately to write and illustrate several advertisements for Flit. Before long, he was working full-time at the job, and his salary swelled to twelve thousand dollars a year, which was a lot of money at the time. The phrase, "Quick Henry, the Flit!" which appeared in the ads, was repeated everywhere. Geisel was developing a name for himself.

He still continued working on cartoons and humorous articles, selling them to magazines such as *Life*—a humor magazine that had been published since 1881—and *Vanity Fair.* He also worked on ads for NBC Radio and Ford Motor Company.

In a feature that ran in *Judge* magazine, Geisel's love of word play was apparent. Entitled "Ough! Ough! Or Why I Believe in Simplified Spelling," the article poked fun at the "evils of the 'ough' words."

Geisel claimed that one day he saw "a tough, coughing as he ploughed a field which (being quite near-sighted) I mistook for pie dough.

"Assuming that all "ough" words were pronounced the same, I casually remarked, 'The tuff cuffs as he pluffs the duff!'[3]

Money was plentiful now and the couple was able to afford a nicer apartment. The Geisels also took long vacations all over the world. They visited Greece, Japan, and Africa. They hoped one day to move to the West Coast, and settle in southern California.

During this time, Geisel's mother began to feel unwell. She had frequent headaches and had trouble staying awake. After consulting a brain surgeon, it was discovered that she had a brain tumor. The doctors were not able to remove it, and in 1931, Henrietta Geisel died.

That same year, Geisel was asked if he would be interested in illustrating a book of children's sayings taken from classrooms and test papers. It had originally been published in England as *Schoolboy Howlers.* In America, it was to be called *Boners* and would include Geisel's sketches. The book was very successful and stayed on *The New York Times* best-seller list for nonfiction for two months. *More Boners* appeared less than a year later. Reviewers claimed the success of these books was due to the drawings of Dr. Seuss.

Geisel enjoyed illustrating the books, but he wanted something more. He said he ". . . began to realize that if I hoped to succeed in the book world, I'd have to write, as well as draw."[4]

He came up with an idea for an alphabet book. Geisel filled it with his drawings of strange animals. But he did not know much about the publishing industry and used many different colored inks, which were expensive. Because of the cost, the book was not practical to publish. It would be far too expensive. Although he mailed the manuscript out to some major publishers, no one was interested in buying it.

In 1935, Geisel also created and wrote a comic strip called "Hejji by Dr. Seuss." Geisel had recently visited Peru, the setting of the comic strip. He made up the Land of Baako, where his characters lived in the snow-capped mountains. The creatures were typically Seuss—a pair of goats joined together by a single beard, blue elephants, whales sitting on old volcano tops, happily spouting water high into the air.

Geisel had been hired to do the strip by Hearst newspapers. But a few weeks after he'd begun drawing Hejji, he was one of three people fired.

At this time, Geisel was also working on other advertising projects for Standard Oil, producers of Flit insecticide. He did numerous ads for Essolube 5-Star Motor Oil. His illustrations included grinning monkeys and smiling catlike creatures.

Geisel played with the text of the ads as well as the drawings. He promised that Essolube would, "Foil the

Moto-raspus! Foil the Zero-doccus! Foil the Karbo-nockus!"[5]

It was on one of the couple's many trips that Geisel came up with another idea for a children's book. The year was 1936, and Geisel and Helen were returning from their European travels on the M.S. *Kungsholm.* Geisel wrote down some verses to the beat of the ship's engines in order to take his mind off the storm at sea. The result was *And to Think That I Saw It on Mulberry Street.*

And with that story, Dr. Seuss's career as an author of children's books was launched.

On Mulberry Street

"The 'creative process' consists for me of two things—time and sweat," Geisel once said.[1]

He worked on the manuscript of *And to Think That I Saw It on Mulberry Street* for six months. Every word in the story was rewritten and then rewritten again.

"The agony is terrific at times," he said of the writing process.[2]

Just like his father, Geisel strived for perfection. And *Mulberry Street* was no exception.

The verse that appears in *Mulberry Street*—as well as Geisel's other books—seems simple on the surface.

But according to Geisel, "I'm a bleeder and I sweat at it . . . The difficult thing about writing for kids is that you can write yourself into a box: If you can't get a proper rhyme for a quatrain [four lines of verse], you not only have to throw that quatrain out but you also have to unravel the sock way back, probably 10 pages or so."[3]

Beginning with *Mulberry Street*, the rhythm that Geisel favored in his books is called anapestic tetrameter. Two unstressed syllables are followed by one stressed syllable, as in Clement Moore's poem, "'Twas the Night Before Christmas":

> 'Twas the *night* before *Christ*mas
> When *all* through the *house*
> Not a *crea*ture was *stir*ring
> Not *e*ven a *mouse*.

This is the rhythm Geisel heard in the ship's engines as he wrote *Mulberry Street*. It is a rhythm that has a lot of energy and excitement:

> AND TO *THINK* THAT I *SAW* IT
> ON *MULBERRY STREET!*[4]

The flowing verse, the engaging storyline, and Geisel's cartoonlike animals all made *Mulberry Street* an instant success. Book reviewers praised the story. One review in particular remained Geisel's favorite throughout his life. It ran in *The New Yorker* magazine on Nov. 6, 1937, and was written by Clifton Fadiman:

> *They say it's for children, but better get a copy for yourself and marvel at the good Dr. Seuss' impossible pictures and the moral tale of the little boy who exaggerated not wisely but too well.*[5]

The 'moral tale' of *Mulberry Street* tells of a young

Despite Geisel's success, he was more comfortable at home than in the public eye. He is pictured here with his wife, Helen, at their California home.

boy named Marco who wants to have something interesting to relate to his father about what he's seen on his walk home from school. Unfortunately, all Marco notices is a horse-drawn wagon.

Marco realizes that if a zebra were pulling the wagon, it would be far more interesting. Before long the zebra becomes a reindeer who turns into a blue elephant flanked by two giraffe-like creatures. By the time Marco returns home, he has added a big brass band, confetti pouring down from an airplane, policemen on motorcycles, a magician pulling rabbits from a hat, and much more.

Yet even though Marco flies excitedly up the steps

after school and is anxious to see his father, he has a change of heart at the last minute. When his father asks Marco what he saw on his walk home, Marco replies that he merely saw a horse and wagon walking along Mulberry Street.

Originally rejected by nearly thirty publishers, the criticism and praise of *Mulberry Street* were the same—it was different. Children's literature at that time focused on the text, not the illustrations. Yet Geisel's book had the text and pictures working together to tell the story. His drawings helped young children follow the story even if they could not yet read.

Mulberry Street was also unusual in that it did not preach or talk down to children. The English author Beatrix Potter, who created *Peter Rabbit*, praised the book for its "natural truthful simplicity of the untruthfulness."[6]

Although the cost of one dollar was expensive for a book at that time, *Mulberry Street* rapidly sold more than ten thousand copies.

The success of the book put Geisel in the limelight. He was asked to give a speech at a women's college in Westchester, New York. Always nervous about appearing in public, Geisel did not want to travel to New York. But Helen urged him to accept the invitation. The crowd at the college waited two hours before realizing Geisel was not going to show up. When Geisel returned home that night, he admitted to Helen that he had sat in the train station the entire afternoon. He had not been able to force himself to speak in public.

"I don't like audiences. I prefer to make my mistakes in private," Geisel once said. "I enjoy giving a one-on-one interview, but I do not like being on a platform; it makes me very nervous and uncomfortable."[7]

The success of *Mulberry Street* encouraged Geisel to write another children's book. One year after *Mulberry Street*, Vanguard Press published *The 500 Hats of Bartholomew Cubbins*.

Geisel said he got the idea for the story as he was riding a train one morning. The man sitting in front of him looked as if he worked on Wall Street, New York City's financial district. The man was wearing a suit, a tie, and a hat. Geisel began to wonder what the man would do if Geisel were to grab the hat and throw it out the window. Geisel decided the man would probably just grow another hat.

That became the basis for *The 500 Hats of Bartholomew Cubbins*, a story about a boy who has hats grow on top of his head just as quickly as he can remove them.

The book was different from *Mulberry Street* in that the text was not in verse. The story itself was actually a fairy tale.

"I knew nothing about children's books," Geisel said. ". . . Traditional fairy tales were still in order. I thought perhaps that was the thing to do."[8]

As with *Mulberry Street*, Geisel demanded perfection from himself when writing *The 500 Hats*. He worked intensely on the book and spoke frequently on the telephone with his editor, asking for changes to be made to the manuscript.

In one change, Geisel originally planned for Bartholomew to only have forty-eight hats, but the number quickly grew to five hundred. Geisel, in fact, possessed his own collection of several hundred hats. He owned everything from a fireman's hat from Ecuador to a Czechoslovakian helmet to an admiral's hat in the British Navy.

Reviewers praised *The 500 Hats.* Seuss's zany cartoon-like drawings and engaging story seemed to combine the best of a comic strip with a Grimm Brothers fairy tale.

Geisel dedicated the book to Chrysanthemum-Pearl, a child borne out of his imagination. Geisel and Helen never did have a family of their own. Helen had needed surgery in the early years of their marriage and was unable to have children. Geisel always said that he had no special love for children. He said he felt about children the way he felt about adults—some he liked and some he did not.

In response to questions about why he did not have children, Geisel was fond of saying, "You have 'em, I'll amuse 'em."[9]

Shortly after the publication of *The 500 Hats*, Geisel began working on an idea that had nothing to do with writing or illustrating. It was an invention.

The Infantograph was the creation of Geisel and his partner Ralph Warren. This special camera would photograph a man and a woman at the same time, and the resulting picture would predict what the couple's child would look like. Although the men patented the device, it was a failure. The baby's face came out with either crooked features, a mustache, or some other problem.

Geisel had hoped to display the Infantograph at the 1939 World's Fair in New York City. But the invention did not make its debut in New York or anywhere else.

Geisel and Helen visited the World's Fair that year, in spite of the Infantograph's failure. Geisel's niece Peggy, age eleven, stayed with them for a week. With no children of their own, the couple was very close to Peggy. She slept in Ted's studio and when Geisel could take a break from work, they would go over to the fairgrounds.

Geisel now had two successful children's books behind him. Random House publisher Bennett Cerf hoped to convince Geisel to leave Vanguard Press and come to his publishing house.

The men met and instantly got along. Geisel realized that Random House was a larger company than Vanguard and would be able to market his books more effectively. Random House could also offer its writers more money.

Cerf was so anxious to have Geisel join Random House that he offered the writer complete freedom over his next project. Random House would print whatever Geisel wrote, Cerf promised.

Geisel decided to try a book for adults. *The Seven Lady Godivas* was published in 1939 and was a huge failure. Set in the eleventh century, the book tells the humorous story of seven sisters who cannot marry the seven Peeping brothers until each sister learns a scientific truth about horses. Geisel's drawings are in red, black, and white and show one of Geisel's few attempts to draw humans, instead of animals. Although the text does not rhyme, the story is filled with tongue-in-cheek humor.

He returned to children's literature with *The King's Stilts*. The story is a fairy tale about King Birtram who enjoys playing with a pair of red stilts. But one day, the stilts are stolen and the kingdom nearly falls to ruin.

Geisel worked as diligently on this manuscript as he had with the others. Helen worked with him, assisting her husband with editing the text. For the illustrations, Geisel did pencil sketches and jotted down notes as to how the pictures should be drawn. The book did better than *The Seven Lady Godivas*, but it was not particularly successful.

Geisel soon came up with an idea for another book, this one destined to be an all-time favorite among his readers. It was also the story Geisel would refer to as "the happiest book."[10]

Wartime

Horton Hatches the Egg came to Geisel by accident.

"I was sitting in my studio one day, working on transparent tracing paper, and the window blew open," Geisel said.[1]

The wind lifted the picture of an elephant, which Geisel had just sketched. The paper landed on top of a drawing of a tree.

"All I had to do was figure out what the elephant was doing on that tree," said Geisel.[2]

What Geisel figured out became one of his most popular books. And Horton the elephant was one of Geisel's favorite animal creations.

Horton Hatches the Egg tells the story of a lazy bird named Maysie who persuades Horton to sit on her egg so she can take off on vacation. Horton patiently cares for the egg.

Horton protects the egg from the freezing cold of winter, a terrible storm, and hunters. He remains steadfast even while his friends make fun of him. Horton's reward for his loyalty at the end of the story is the birth of an elephant-bird.

Geisel put in long hours on the book, but he worked quickly. One of the many changes he made as he worked was the name of the elephant. Horton was first named Osmer, then Bosco, then Humphrey. "Horton" was actually the name of a classmate who had attended Dartmouth with Geisel. Mayzie the bird was initially Bessie, then Saidie.

Geisel was sure it was well written, funny, and had an interesting story line that would appeal to children. In a letter to a friend, Geisel wrote, "Never before have I stood before myself and pointed so proudly, saying, "Genius, you are." I feel certain it will sell well over a million . . ."[3]

Although Geisel was correct in predicting the book's popularity, he was not in earnest when referring to himself as a genius. He believed that his success was based on hard work: "If I were a genius, why do I have to sweat so hard at my work? I know my stuff all looks like it was rattled off in twenty-three seconds, but every word is a struggle and every sentence is like the pangs of birth."[4]

Success came instantly. And it was the first of Geisel's books to include a moral. "I seldom start with one [moral]," Geisel said, "but when you write a kid's book, somebody's got to win. You find yourself preaching in spite of yourself."[5]

By using humor and making a concerted effort not to sound preachy, Geisel's message was delivered lightly. "I don't write for children, I write for people," he once said. "Once a writer starts talking down to kids, he's lost. Kids can pick up on that kind of thing."[6]

Bennett Cerf was so pleased with the manuscript from the moment he saw it, that he gave Geisel a large advance of five hundred dollars.

In spite of the success of *Horton Hatches the Egg*, the 37-year-old Geisel soon found himself distracted by the political events at that time. World War II began in 1939 and lasted until 1945. The two sides were known as the Allies—the United States, Great Britain, and France—against the Axis—Germany, Italy, and Japan.

Geisel felt strongly about supporting America's involvement in the war against Adolf Hitler, Germany's dictator. In 1941, Geisel drew a cartoon for *PM* magazine, aimed at American aviator Charles Lindbergh. Lindbergh had been the first person to make a nonstop solo flight across the Atlantic Ocean in 1927, and he had become a national hero.

But ten years later, when Lindbergh allowed the German government to honor him for his achievements, many people—including Geisel—were highly critical. Geisel drew a cartoon showing an ostrich with its head buried in the sand. That was the first of many cartoons Geisel would create for *PM*.

In 1942, Geisel joined the United States Army. He

became part of the Information and Education Division and worked with Academy Award-winning director Frank Capra in Hollywood, California.

The Geisels had already been spending time in California. With this army commission, they now decided to close out their apartment in New York City.

During the day, Geisel spent his time at the Hollywood Studio. He helped produce animated cartoons aimed at training the men in military service. By working with Capra on film scripts, Geisel learned even more about the writing process. Capra showed him how to keep a story moving along and how to get rid of the parts that didn't help advance the plot. Capra would use a blue pencil to underline the sections of a manuscript that told the story or hastened the plot.

"I've tried to ensure that the majority of my manuscripts merited blue pencil marks," Geisel said.[7] This way, he would be certain that he was not using unnecessary words.

Helen, meanwhile, was working on children's books of her own. Writing for Disney and Golden Books, she turned out *Tommy's Wonderful Rides, Donald Duck Sees South America, Bobby and His Airplane*, and *Johnny's Machines*.

As the war continued and Geisel's writing and editing skills improved, Capra gave him longer projects to work on. Occasionally, Geisel had to travel to Washington, D.C., where he had meetings at the War Department.

Geisel was asked to fly to England and France. He took with him the reels for the film he had written

THE PLEASURE IS ALL OURS!

7 MILLION NEW U.S. TAX-PAYERS

Dr. Seuss

Drawn especially for the Treasury Department's War Tax Program....

Geisel drew many political cartoons during World War II including this sketch showing America's attitude toward Germany and Japan. Pictured here is Hitler and an unnamed Japanese leader.

called, *Your Job in Germany.* The live-action film was directed at Allied soldiers who would be occupying Germany at the end of the war. It warned the Allies not to trust the Germans or befriend any of the German people.

In 1945, Geisel returned to the United States. Joyful as he was to see the end of World War II, he was grief-stricken at the unexpected death of his sister Marnie. She died in September of that year from a heart attack. Geisel was so deeply affected by her death that he was unable to talk about it for the rest of his life.

The following year, Geisel left the army. He was awarded the Legion of Merit for his work on the animated cartoons that helped inform and train the troops. He also won two Academy Awards for documentary features. One, in 1946, for *Hitler Lives* (called *Your Job in Germany*) and the other, in 1947, for *Design for Death.* This film was written with his wife and told the history of the Japanese people.

The Geisels remained in California after the war. They eventually moved to La Jolla in 1948, where they had dreamed of living years earlier.

Geisel had enjoyed working on films, but book writing would always be his preference. He soon got to work on his first book in seven years, *McElligot's Pool.*

His only book to be illustrated in watercolors, *McElligot's Pool* tells the story of a young boy who goes fishing in McElligot's Pool. The pool is really nothing more than a puddle where people have thrown their junk. But in a style similar to *Mulberry Street,* the boy begins to imagine all the wonderful fish that just might lie beneath the water. If the pool is deeper than anyone thinks, it might connect to an underground stream, and many different fish might be swimming there. There might be fish that look like flowers and others that have a head at both ends. Throughout the story, the boy dreams of an odd and often nonsensical assortment of fish that might be swimming beneath the water.

Widely praised for its artistry, *McElligot's Pool* was a Caldecott Honor book in 1948. The Caldecott medal is given annually to the artist who creates the most distinguished picture book for children published in the United States. It is named after Randolph J. Caldecott, a nineteenth-century English illustrator. Caldecott Honor books are runners-up for the medal.

This came about in spite of the fact that Random House would only publish every other pair of facing pages in color because of the expense.

It was Geisel's most elaborate book artistically.

"I've never had any formal [art] instruction, and I really can't draw at all, not in the artistic sense. But I know something about color, I think, and I like to get three-dimensional effects with paintings that aren't for publication," Geisel said.[8]

Yet Geisel never again returned to the subtle watercolor tones of *McElligot's Pool.*

"A child's idea of art is a pen-and-ink drawing filled in with flat color," he said. "That's just the way kids see things."[9]

When Geisel was forty-four, he and Helen bought an observation tower sitting on six and one-half acres in La Jolla. Geisel turned the upper tower into his studio. He was able to look down on the Pacific Ocean. If the sky was clear, he could see seventy-five miles (120 kilometers) out to sea from his perch.

He used a drafting table as his desk and would sit down at it by ten each morning. Regularly putting in eight-hour days, Geisel doodled or sketched in total silence. He would sit in a swivel chair and occasionally pace the length of the studio. He was also a chain smoker.

Despite his strict work hours, Geisel claimed he did his best writing and illustrating late at night when he was slightly tired.

McElligot's Pool began a wave of Dr. Seuss books. In 1948, he wrote *Thidwick the Big-Hearted Moose*, a story of a moose whose generous nature results in a variety of animals nesting in his antlers.

Just as *Horton Hatches the Egg* came about by accident, Geisel claimed *Thidwick* had similar roots. He had been sitting in front of his typewriter, trying to come up with a story idea for a movie. He was unable to think of anything and continued staring at the blank sheet of paper. When the telephone rang, Geisel recalled pulling the paper out of the typewriter and sketching "absent-minded, meaningless scribbles" while he talked to his friend Joe Warwick.

"It wasn't until after Joe had hung up that I realized that one of the scribbles looked somewhat like a moose, with some other peculiar animals sitting on his horns," Geisel said. "Then I began to wonder how a moose would like it if some animals did move in to live on his horns."[10]

By the time Geisel published McElligot's Pool, *he had become a favorite author among children. Shown here at Dartmouth College in 1962, he was surrounded by his fans.*

Geisel had originally named the moose "Warwick," in honor of his friend. As he worked on the book, the name evolved into "Thidwick."

The idea for Geisel's next book came from a comment he had heard a soldier make one rainy night in Belgium during World War II. "Rain, always rain. Why can't we have something different for a change?"[11]

Bartholomew and the Oobleck was published in 1949. In the story, King Derwin of Didd is bored by the sun, fog, rain, and snow. He asks his magicians to come up with something new that can fall from the sky. The magicians create oobleck. But the green, gloppy mess causes such problems in the kingdom that the king is forced to say his own magic words—"I'm sorry"—in order to make it stop.

Explaining how he came up with the strange names of his animals and locations, Geisel once joked, "Why, I've been to most of these places myself so the names are from memory. As for the animals, I have a special dictionary which gives most of them, and I just look up the spellings."[12]

Bartholomew and the Oobleck, along with *If I Ran the Zoo* (1950) and *Scrambled Eggs Super!* (1953) were very successful. Both *Bartholomew and the Oobleck* and *If I Ran the Zoo* were named Caldecott Honor books. And as always, Geisel claimed the ideas for the stories did not come from any specific source.

His ideas would "always start as a doodle," he said. "I may doodle a couple of animals; if they bite each other, it's going to be a good book. If you doodle enough, the characters begin to take over themselves. . . ."

Geisel returned briefly to filmmaking when he wrote the script for *Gerald McBoing-Boing*. He did not draw the illustrations because he had never thought he was very good at drawing humans, so someone else drew the pictures.

Gerald McBoing-Boing won the Academy Award for best animated cartoon in 1951. It tells the story of a young boy who is unable to speak. Instead, he makes different sounds like the neigh of a horse or the creak of a door. Because everyone makes fun of him, Gerald runs away. He is discovered by a talent scout and lands a job doing sound effects on the radio.

Geisel also worked on a live-action movie called *The 5,000 Fingers of Dr. T*. He sold his story idea to Columbia Studios. The movie was about the evil Dr. Terwilliker who lives in a castle with a two-story-high piano keyboard. The doctor forces hundreds of boys to play the piano continuously. If they stop, the boys get thrown into a dungeon. Bart, the ten-year-old hero of the film, rebels against Dr. Terwilliker and saves the boys.

The making of the film did not go smoothly. Production was continually postponed, the budget had to be cut, and various changes were made in the script. When Geisel said he was withdrawing from the film, he was told that the scenes he did not like would be removed.

Geisel recalled one particularly eventful day where the boys who were playing the part of the imprisoned pianists ate hot dogs for lunch. One by one, nearly every boy became sick and threw up on his keyboard.

"When the picture was finally released, the critics reacted in much the same manner," Geisel remembered.

Unlike *Gerald McBoing-Boing*, Geisel's newest film was a total failure. Most audiences left their seats long before *The 5,000 Fingers of Dr. T* movie had ended. Geisel remembered the film's debut in 1953 as the worst night of his life.

Putting his disappointment behind him, Geisel set to work on a second book about Horton the elephant.

He called it *Horton Hears 'Em!* at first, then changed the title to *Horton Hears a Who!*

As usual, Helen worked closely with her husband on the manuscript. And as usual, Geisel aimed for perfection, working and reworking the words until they had the right flow and rhythm. Describing Horton's attempts to find the tiny Whos in a field of clover, Geisel initially wrote that the elephant:

> *had plucked nineteen thousand four hundred and five.*

Then he wrote:

> *had piled up twelve thousand nine hundred five.*

And in his final version:

> *had picked, searched, and piled up, nine thousand and five.*

Bennett Cerf praised the story of Horton, the elephant who hears a tiny cry for help from a speck of dust:

> *I'll just have to save him. Because, after all,*
> *A person's a person, no matter how small.*[13]

Horton searches for and finds the Whos. He carefully puts the dust speck on clover to protect the Whos. But then an eagle carries the clover away, and Horton must again search for the little creatures. He is able to find them by encouraging the Whos to make as much noise as they can.

Cerf correctly predicted that Dr. Seuss had created another success. Illustrations from the book were used in an exhibition presented by the New York Public Library. It was highly praised by both *The New York Herald Tribune* and *The Des Moines Register* newspapers.

Yet Geisel's biggest triumph was still to come.

8

The Cat in the Hat Is Born

In the spring of 1954, Helen was stricken with a paralysis of her body. It was diagnosed as Guillain-Barré syndrome, a nervous disorder that results in the weakness of the legs, arms, breathing muscles, and face. Paralysis is common, and it was not certain that she would survive.

Helen was unable to walk, talk, or even swallow. She needed to spend time in an iron lung, a device that surrounds a person's chest and "breathes" for them, forcing air into and out of the lungs. She remained in the iron lung until the middle of the summer.

Slowly, over the course of a year, Helen began to improve. She exercised and learned how to do the simplest tasks, such as combing her hair or brushing her teeth. However, she would suffer from stiffness in her legs and feet for the rest of her life.

At this time, Geisel, who generally shied away from anything religious, wrote a children's prayer. It was published in *Colliers* magazine on December 23, 1954.

Helen's daily improvement encouraged Geisel to undertake one of his most imaginative books, *On Beyond Zebra,* published in 1955. In this story, the author goes beyond the twenty-six-letter alphabet, creating new letters that go beyond Z.

Geisel came up with elaborate symbols represented by unusual sounds to introduce his new alphabet.

In the spring of that year, Helen was well enough to accompany her husband to Dartmouth College where he was presented with an honorary doctorate degree. Geisel was a respected name in children's literature by the mid-1950s. And finally, thirty years after graduating from college, the "Dr." in his name was legitimate.

College president John Sloan Dickey said of Geisel's work at the presentation, ". . . As always with the best of humor, behind the fun there has been intelligence, kindness, and a feel for humankind."[1]

Geisel worked hard to make his books enjoyable for children. But some reading experts felt that the books used in schools to teach reading skills were boring.

In 1956, an article in *Life* magazine suggested that many American children were having difficulty learning how to read because the books for beginning readers were not interesting. The author of the article was John Hersey. He suggested that children would be more motivated to read if the process were fun for them. Why couldn't someone like Dr. Seuss write the books? Why shouldn't beginning reading books have "drawings like those wonderfully imaginative geniuses among children's illustrators, Tenniel, Howard Pyle, 'Dr. Seuss,' Walt Disney?"[2]

William Spaulding, director of the education division at Houghton Mifflin publishers, read the article. He contacted Geisel, begging him to come to Boston. Spaulding suggested that Geisel write a book for beginning readers. Geisel accepted the challenge. He was given a list of words and told to take it home and "play with it."[3]

"At first I thought it was impossible and ridiculous, and I was about to get out of the whole thing," Geisel said, "then [I] decided to look at the list one more time and to use the first two words that rhymed as the title of the book."[4]

The words Geisel saw were "cat" and "hat." And for the next nine months, he worked on the manuscript.

Geisel was actually given three lists in all. The first list contained 220 words, which the reading experts believed most young children would be able to recognize. Geisel used 123 of these words, such as "a," "about," "and," "ball," "come," and "house."

The next list provided 220 words which a beginning reader might not have encountered, but which he would probably be able to sound out. For example, if a child knew "make," he would most likely be able to sound out "cake" and "rake." This list included "cat," "tall," "book," and "bit." Geisel used forty-five of them.

The final list was composed of words an early reader might never have seen before, but would most likely be able to understand. These 200 words included: "beat," "fear," and "kick." Geisel chose thirty-one.[5]

The work did not come easily. Always the perfectionist, he often threw the manuscript across the room out of frustration. He had expected to write the manuscript in two or three weeks. Yet the task took him more than a year.

Geisel was beloved by young readers because his books encouraged their imaginations. He is shown signing books on "Dr. Seuss Day" in 1962 at Dartmouth College.

"You try telling a complicated story using less than two hundred and fifty words!" he said. "The story has to develop clearly and logically with a valid problem and a valid solution. The characters . . . have to be vivid and believable and consistent. Then I have to get illustrations that fit the text and don't destroy the mood. The whole affect has to be just right."[6]

He felt a fast-paced tempo was crucial and played with the words to achieve that end. For example, he originally wrote the line:

He fell off the ball.

Geisel then changed it to:

He came down from the ball.

Finally, he wrote:

He came down with a bump from up there on the ball.[7]

The text was not all he struggled with. He was also painstaking with his illustrations. He wanted his cat to be clever without being mean. He wanted him to be a troublemaker, but in an innocent way.

The result was *The Cat in the Hat*, a story of a brother and sister who are stuck indoors on a cold, wet day. Their boredom is alleviated by a mischievous cat and his two helpers, Thing One and Thing Two. After the cat's antics make a mess of the house, he cleans everything up with the help of a magical machine.

While the story is fantasy, Geisel typically made even the illogical seem believable. "If I start out with the concept of a two-headed animal," he once explained, "I must put two hats on his head and two toothbrushes in the bathroom. It's logical insanity."[8]

When the book was published in the spring of 1957, the following article appeared in *The New York Times*:

"Talk about making bricks without straw and omelets without eggs! Anyone around here tried writing a book without words? Well, not quite without any words. . .

"Ted Geisel tried. And he did it."[9]

The Cat in the Hat was more successful than anything Geisel had previously written. John Hersey later called the book a "gift to the art of reading."[10]

In fact, Random House was so excited by the book's sales, that it launched a new division of children's books, calling it the Beginner Book series. Many of these books would be written by Geisel, but other authors—such as P. D. Eastman—also contributed. Occasionally, Geisel would write the text but hire another illustrator to do the drawings. When this occurred, he wrote under the name Theo LeSieg (Geisel spelled backward).

There have been a few criticisms of *The Cat in the Hat*. They can generally be traced to the cat's flaunting of authority and what appears to be Geisel's approval of it. But for the most part, the book has been widely praised. Its simple, easy-to-follow story line, the flowing verse, and the bold illustrations have won millions of fans.

According to Susan Mandel Glazer, professor of graduate studies at Rider University, some educators were uncomfortable with the book "because they didn't like putting fantasy in kids' heads. In those times, reality was more important than fantasy."[11]

Yet Glazer said there was a major problem with the Dick and Jane primers—characters in a series of learn-to-read books that were popular in classrooms in the 1950s. Glazer said that they focused solely on teaching word recognition. Understanding the content of the books was considered separate, and there was no attempt to teach it.

"But Dr. Seuss has a story. He pulls you in," Glazer said. "His talent for playing with language is what pulls you in . . . And the interesting part of Dr. Seuss is that his language is so rhythmic and humorous, that adults like it as well."

Geisel purposely began the story using the simplest, most familiar language.

He said he used such basic words, "so that the reader, recognizing it, can sound out similar words."[12]

Just as easily as the Cat balances a dozen different objects, the reader makes his way through the simple rhymes.

Over a period of three years, nearly a million copies of *The Cat in the Hat* were sold, including editions in Chinese, Swedish, French, and Braille. *The Cat in the Hat* would always be the book Geisel was proudest of.

"I feel my greatest accomplishment was getting rid of Dick and Jane and encouraging students to approach reading as a pleasure, not a chore," Geisel said.[13]

The Cat would continue to pop up in *The Cat in the*

Hat Comes Back (1958), *The Cat in the Hat Songbook* (1967), *The Cat's Quizzer* (1976), and *I Can Read with My Eyes Shut* (1978).

The Cat in the Hat Comes Back once again features Sally and her brother, only this time, they must shovel snow. The Cat in the Hat arrives and decides to eat cake in their tub. He leaves a big stain, which he has to clean. But the stain tends to travel to objects throughout the house until the Cat must ask little cats from inside his hat to help with the job.

The Cat in the Hat Song Book features nineteen songs by Geisel and a full piano score by Eugene Poddany. The lively songs with their humorous lyrics

Geisel's characters and machines have become recognizable around the world. This ice sculpture was built at Dartmouth College in 1981.

include "Super-Supper March" and "Lullaby for Mr. Benjamin B. Bickelbaum."

The Cat's Quizzer is a book of silly questions such as "Do roosters sleep on their backs or sides?" and "Do pineapples grow on pine or apple trees?" *I Can Read with My Eyes Shut* shows the Cat in the Hat reading in many different ways—including with his eyes closed—until he discovers how much easier it is to read with his eyes open.

The Cat would become Geisel's most famous creation. And throughout his career, Geisel would keep a larger-than-life canvas of the Cat grinning at him from his studio wall.

More Stories

The year 1957 was a banner year for Geisel. Not only was *The Cat in the Hat* starting off with sales of twelve thousand copies a month, but *How the Grinch Stole Christmas!* was published, and it quickly became one of his most popular books.

Geisel would later say that the book was his easiest to write. The Grinch, a typically unidentifiable Seuss creature, hates Christmas. He tries to prevent it from arriving in Who-ville by stealing all the gifts, food, and decorations. But the Grinch is shocked to find that the Whos still are celebrating on Christmas morning.

Geisel was extremely proud of the book's illustrations. But he had a problem figuring out how to end the story. He needed to get "the Grinch out of the mess," yet he wanted to avoid preaching, as well as delivering any kind of religious message.[1]

Finally, he decided to have the Whos and the Grinch sit down together to Christmas dinner.

English professor Ruth MacDonald believed that the Grinch was actually a reflection of Geisel himself (his license plate read "Grinch"). In the story, Geisel mentioned that the Grinch had been tolerating the Whos' Christmas festivities for fifty-three years—Geisel's own age in 1957.

Also, Geisel had long hated noisy celebrations and blatant materialism. He did not like people focusing more on the gifts than on the meaning behind the holidays. He made sure not to be home on his birthday because he did not want to deal with the numerous children who came with songs and cards to his house. In the story, Geisel's message is the importance of the holiday spirit, not the superficial trappings that go with it.

Geisel was careful not to "hit them [children] over the head with the moral . . . you have to work it in sideways. But it has to be there," he said. "If the Grinch steals Christmas, as he does in one of my books, he has to bring it back in the end. I must say, though, when I was doing that one I was kind of rooting for the Grinch."[2]

The *Grinch* was a success from the moment it appeared in stores. Thanks in part to Geisel, Random House became the largest children's book publisher in the country that year. And riding on the heels of *The Cat in the Hat*'s success, The *Grinch* pushed

Geisel firmly into a celebrity role where he would remain for the rest of his life.

Although he still intensely disliked appearing in public, Geisel agreed to attend various events where he would autograph books. When *Yertle the Turtle* and *The Cat in the Hat Comes Back* appeared the following year, he traveled to bookstores from Boston to Chicago, signing books for fans.

Because of his fame, other events were held that kept Geisel in the limelight. Teachers in Rochester, New York proclaimed a Dr. Seuss Day and asked the author to be present. Geisel appeared on the television game show, *To Tell the Truth*. In Washington, D.C., workers at the zoo were asked to study Geisel's animals. There seemed to be no end of Dr. Seuss events.

During this time, Geisel and Helen continued working on the Beginner Books series. Often, they had huge problems with the quality of the books that were to be included in the series. They did not like the illustrations in P. D. Eastman's *Sam and the Firefly*; they considered them of poor quality. They also objected to the text of *You Will Go to the Moon* by Mae and Ira Freeman. Helen wrote a letter for her husband, saying, "Before any illustrator can breathe any life into this story with pictures, the authors have got to first breathe some life into it with words. . . ."[3]

Geisel and his wife were as much perfectionists when editing the Beginner Books as Geisel was when writing on his own.

He had also begun working with a company to

Geisel worked with a company to create Dr. Seuss toys. Here Geisel is shown holding a stuffed Cat in the Hat doll.

produce Dr. Seuss animal toys—including the Cat in the Hat and Horton. Geisel was earning more money than he had dreamed possible. In 1959, he was the highest-paid author in the world for that year, earning about $200,000.

Yet Geisel was not particularly interested in money. And he refused to accept money for something he did not believe in.

He was once offered a large sum of money if he would let a television advertiser use a short verse of his in a holiday advertisement. Geisel said no. The advertiser offered him even more money. Geisel still refused.

His agent, Herbert Cheyette, said to him, "If you accept this deal you will go down into *The Guinness Book of Records* as the writer who was paid the most money per word."[4]

Geisel's response was, "I'd rather go into *The Guinness Book of Records* as the writer who refused to be paid the most money per word."[5] Geisel rarely spent much money and he made fun of the lawyers who were in charge of his finances. He made up a law firm entitled, "Grimalkin, Drouberhannus, Knalber and Fepp" and claimed he would be lost without their helpful advice.[6]

Yet the books—and the money—kept coming. In 1959, Random House published *Happy Birthday to You!* And in 1960, *One Fish Two Fish Red Fish Blue Fish* and *Green Eggs and Ham* appeared. That year, Beginner Books topped a million dollars in sales.

In writing *One Fish Two Fish*, Geisel was aiming at an even lower reading level than *The Cat in the Hat.*

The language was simpler than anything Geisel had used before. Yet the author still tried to open children's minds to the idea that the world was a fun and exciting place. It became one of the most popular books in the Beginner Books series.

Geisel wrote *Green Eggs and Ham* in order to win a bet. He had already written successful books with two hundred-odd words. Now, Bennett Cerf challenged Geisel to write a book using only fifty words. The winner would receive fifty dollars. Geisel was determined to win and set out to write the book.

Green Eggs and Ham contains fifty different words (although Geisel claimed he never actually received the fifty dollars). It tells of Sam-I-am, an inventive creature who tries everything hc can think of to coax a nameless character into trying green eggs and ham.

Geisel made numerous lists and charts as he wrote the book. He used the word "not" eighty-two times and "I" eighty-one times. The only word containing more than one syllable was "anywhere," which was used eight times.

In a National Education Association poll of favorite children's books, *Green Eggs and Ham* ranked third in the year 2000. Because of the book's huge success, Geisel was frequently served green eggs when he would attend banquets.

Now in his mid-fifties, Geisel began working on *The Sneetches and Other Stories*. Delivering a message against prejudice, *The Sneetches* relates the tale of plain-bellied Sneetches and the higher status Sneetches who have stars on their bellies.

Helen worked hard keeping visitors away from her husband so he could write in peace. The creative process had not gotten easier for Geisel over the years. He usually worked on two different books at the same time. If he got stuck on one book, he would simply switch to the other. He would also wear any of the various hats in his collection as a thinking cap to help him out.

And yet, in spite of these efforts, he claimed that 99 percent of what he wrote wound up in the wastebasket. For every book Geisel finished, he said he discarded enough material to fill thirty-five others.

Geisel was frequently asked to do signings for children.

The process was no easier with his illustrations. "There are millions of figures—drawings, kids, clothes—which haunt me because I can't seem to do anything about them," he said, "dozens of ideas which never have jelled."[7]

Helen was also busily at work. When the couple flew to New York to give *The Sneetches* to Random House, Helen was finishing her Beginner Book, *A Fish Out of Water.*

After Geisel wrote *Dr. Seuss's Sleep Book* in 1962, he concentrated on the Beginner Books. That same year, *Dr. Seuss's ABC* and *Hop on Pop* were published. And the critics raved.

"As for Dr. Seuss, that wizard is bent on removing reading frustrations before they start. . . The illustrations are as funny as ever; they also provide clues for figuring out the meaning of words. Dr. Seuss thinks of everything."[8]

Geisel returned to writing for a higher reading level with *I Had Trouble in Getting to Solla Sollew* in 1965. Book reviewers praised the story about a creature who is constantly plagued by troubles, so he sets out in search of a place where fewer problems exist.

The journey, however, presents problems of its own. Strange animals attack him along the bumpy, rocky road.

At the conclusion of the story, the creature decides to deal with his troubles instead of running away from them.

At this time, Geisel was approached about making a television adaptation of one of his books. At first, he was not interested. He could still clearly recall the failure of *The 5,000 Fingers of Dr. T.* But after listening to the ideas of some people who worked at MGM Studio, Geisel agreed. Because it was hoped to have the show ready for Christmas, *How the Grinch Stole Christmas!* was the book that would be used.

Adapting the *Grinch* for television was an arduous process. Geisel was asked to make the color of the Grinch's eyes green instead of black, white, and pink. The television producers thought green would look more evil. He also needed to work on lyrics for the songs. Most importantly, he had to expand on various scenes in the book, since the show was to last half an hour while the book only took twelve minutes to read out loud.

Approximately twenty-five thousand drawings were needed for the show. The drawings of the Grinch, Max, and the Whos were so precise that a viewer could understand exactly what was happening even without the sound.

The show first aired December 18, 1966. It was well received and also helped boost sales of the book. Geisel was receiving nearly two thousand fan letters a week and had long since stopped worrying about his financial situation.

But Geisel was now to experience a great sorrow. On Oct. 23, 1967, Helen died. She had had health problems for years. A memorial service was held for Helen at the La Jolla Museum of Art. The art-reference library at the museum was named the Helen Palmer Geisel Library. The following year, in December, Geisel's father died.

Geisel dealt with his grief by focusing on his work. *The Foot Book* was published in 1968. Using the simplest of language, Geisel explored the world of opposites through feet.

With an even lower reading level than the Beginner Books, *The Foot Book* was the first of the Bright and Early Books published by Random House.

Geisel remarried on August 5, 1968. His new wife was Audrey Dimond. She had been friends with both Helen and Ted for many years. Audrey had two teenaged daughters who spent some time at their new home. But for most of the year, they attended board-ing school.

Ted and Audrey Geisel traveled together, visiting such places as Cambodia, India, and Israel. When they returned from their travels in 1969, *I Can Lick 30 Tigers Today! and Other Stories* was published.

After working on *I Can Draw It Myself* and *Mr. Brown Can Moo! Can You?*, Geisel became interested in writing a book that addressed his environmental concerns. Yet he could not find a way to make the book amusing enough to appeal to children. Realizing he was stuck, Geisel proposed a visit to Kenya in 1970.

One day, Geisel found himself at the Mount Kenya Safari Club. He was sitting at the pool and suddenly looked up. He saw a herd of elephants making their way across the mountains. The idea for a story instantly sprang into his mind.

"I had nothing but a laundry list with me, and I grabbed it," he said. "I wrote ninety percent of the book that afternoon."[9]

By 1975, when this picture was taken, Dr. Seuss (on the right) was the most noted children's author worldwide. He is pictured here with his second wife, Audrey, (center) and Dartmouth Dean of Libraries, Edward C. Lathem (left).

Back home, Geisel worked on his sketches of the Truffula trees, which were based on the trees of the Serengeti Desert.

As for the book's main character, Geisel experimented until he found what he wanted. At first, the character was large, then he was reduced to the size of a gopher. Geisel made him green, then he made him mechanized. In the end, he was a short, elderly creature with a large mustache. Now all the author needed was a name for it. But that part was easy, Geisel said.

He looked exactly like a Lorax.

Final Days

*T*he *Lorax* was not the first book Geisel had written to deliver a serious message. In 1958, the story of *Yertle the Turtle* had been based on Hitler's attempt at world domination. *The Sneetches and Other Stories* appeared in 1961 and discussed racism.

What set *The Lorax* apart from these books, however, was that its message of keeping the land, water, and air clean was still very much a current and highly discussed topic. But the question was raised: Was this book intended for children or adults?

"I try to treat the child as an equal and go on the assumption that a child can understand anything that is read to him if the writer takes care to state it clearly and simply enough," Geisel said.[1]

In telling the story of the Lorax, Geisel warned the reader of the consequences of pollution and discussed the causes of it. A character called the Once-ler destroys the Truffula Forest in order to produce Thneeds. The Lorax, who says he speaks for the trees, continually warns the Once-ler about the dangers of his destruction. By the end of the story, all that remains is the seed of a Truffula tree. And it is up to a child to plant the seed and help rebuild the future.

The book wound up being Geisel's favorite, although it was one of the hardest for him to write. He knew what he wanted to say, but the words were coming out too angrily. Geisel had always worked hard to avoid making his stories preachy. Yet in the case of *The Lorax*, he was finding it hard to avoid.

Compared with Geisel's other books, sales of *The Lorax* were not huge. The book had its critics. People in the Northwest who cut down trees for a living were especially critical. A school in Laytonville, California, even attempted to remove the story from its second-grade reading list because of its not-so-subtle attack on the timber industry. But Geisel stated he was not trying to attack one particular industry. Instead, he was concerned about how the world was wasting its natural resources.

The Lorax was published in 1971, but it was not until the 1980s that the book's popularity grew. The country was paying particular attention to the environment during the eighties, and *The Lorax* seemed to speak for the movement.

Geisel was frequently asked whether it was difficult for him to find names for his odd assortment of characters: "I have to say rather disappointingly that it's not hard at all. Thinking up names is the easiest thing I do. I guess maybe I was just born that way."[2]

For the next ten years, Geisel turned out such books as *Marvin K. Mooney Will You Please Go Now?*, *There's a Wocket in My Pocket!*, *Oh! The Thinks You Can Think!*, and *Hunches in Bunches*.

Marvin K. Mooney, Will You Please Go Now? tells the story of a narrator coming up with a number of ways for Marvin K. Mooney to leave. The narrator suggests that Marvin could leave on stilts, by fish, by balloon or broomstick. He does not really care how. He simply wants Marvin to go!

There's a Wocket in My Pocket is a way of introducing young readers to some commonly used household words. *Oh! the Thinks You Can Think!* encourages readers to let their imagination run its course.

Hunches in Bunches addresses the problem of making up one's mind. The boy in the story cannot decide whether he wants to play football, eat pizza, or fly a kite. To help him make up his mind, he is visited by many "hunches," typical Seuss creatures who wear oversized gloves on their heads. The hunches include a Happy Hunch, a Very Odd Hunch, and a Four-Way Hunch. In the end, the boy realizes he is the only one who can make up his mind.

Hunches in Bunches was Geisel's first book in nine years that was not aimed at very young readers. He enjoyed working on it, but the work was interrupted when he had a heart attack.

Geisel was now seventy-seven, and doctors told him what he had known for at least twenty years—he had to quit smoking. He had tried to quit years earlier by planting strawberry seeds in a corncob pipe and simply chewing on the pipe. Now, he pulled out the pipe and planted radish seeds instead. Whenever he found himself craving a cigarette, Geisel watered the seeds with an eyedropper.

Geisel soon began work on a book with a message as vehement as the one he'd addressed in *The Lorax*. Its title was *The Butter Battle Book*.

"All he would tell me about *The Butter Battle Book* was that it was about some people who ate their bread butter side up, and some others who ate their bread butter side down," said Jane Schulman, Random House publisher. "I had no idea that it was a book about nuclear disarmament until he brought it all finished to New York."[3]

Geisel spent eight to ten hours daily on the story. As with *The Lorax*, he went against his usual pattern of writing a book.

"When I start a new book," Geisel once said, "I'll noodle things over and develop some characters. Most of them go in the wastebasket, but a couple get in conflict. Then words begin to come. If I get stuck mentally in a story, I'll draw my way out."[4]

He wrote the text of *The Butter Battle Book* before working on the illustrations. If he considered *The Lorax* his favorite book, he thought *The Butter Battle Book* was his best.

Few reviewers doubted the importance of Geisel's message in the book. Yet once again, many questioned whether the subject of the nuclear arms race was appropriate for young children.

"It is not fashionable to be optimistic about the nuclear arms race," wrote Gloria Goodale in *The Christian Science Monitor*. "But if the future of the world rests with children, shouldn't they learn that, in addition to seeing evil, mankind is capable of averting it as well?"[5]

Random House regarded the book as Geisel's most important. It was published on the author's eightieth birthday in 1984 and tells how the fighting between the Yooks and the Zooks escalated through the years because of their basic disagreement over how to properly eat bread—butter side up, or butter side down.

The Butter Battle Book was a record breaker. It was the only children's book at the time to appear on *The New York Times* best-seller list for six months. Yet reviews continued to be mixed. The book was praised for its treatment of such a serious subject using the Dr. Seuss rhyme. But it was also criticized as being too frightening for children and for not clearly resolving the battle at the end of the story.

That same year, Geisel was awarded the Pulitzer Prize for his contributions to children's literature. This award is named for journalist Joseph Pulitzer and honors achievement in American journalism, literature, and music. Geisel's work of half a century had made an enormous impact on the education of American children, not to mention children's enjoyment of reading. President Ronald Reagan invited Geisel and Audrey to dine at the White House. Geisel recalled with amusement that he had not hired

Reagan, a former actor, forty years earlier to be the narrator for one of his documentary films.

In 1986, Geisel was asked to be the honorary chairman of the Holiday Bowl, a football game held in San Diego, California. Although he originally turned down the invitation, Audrey talked him into it. He appeared at the game—as well as the parade beforehand—wearing a red jacket and a happy smile.

The final book Geisel would write was *Oh, the Places You'll Go!* appearing on bookshelves in 1990. Geisel was aware this would probably be his last book. He was fighting throat cancer and had not been well for several years. He worked laboriously on the story of all the possibilities—good and bad—that people face as they journey through life.

Cathy Goldsmith, executive art director at Random House, flew from New York to California to work with the frail author on the manuscript. A few days after returning home to New York, Goldsmith received a package from Geisel. It contained a small black velvet box. Assuming she would find jewelry inside, Goldsmith opened the box and saw instead a tiny lime.

Geisel had proudly shown Goldsmith his dwarf lime tree when she had been in California. Along with the lime was a note. Geisel told Goldsmith that she had been voted vice president of the orchard and was to be given a one-third share of that year's lime crop. The remaining two-thirds were to go to Geisel and the Cat in the Hat.

The gift was very special to Goldsmith, although

Audrey Geisel makes an appearance in 1999 to help celebrate the new Cat in the Hat Stamp.

not as special as the time she spent working with the author.

"Working with Ted was a lot like reading one of his books," she said. "You had to be prepared for almost anything. Ted did things with words and characters that no one else could. Just about the time that you thought you had it all figured out, boom—he'd turn it all upside down and inside out and make it even better than before."[6]

Although reviewers for *Oh, the Places You'll Go!* were not ecstatic, the book's sales took off. It quickly went onto *The New York Times* best-seller list where it stayed for more than two years.

Geisel was thrilled. "This proves it! I no longer write for children. I write for *people!*"[7]

In fact, he seemed to be writing for everyone. By 1991, his forty-seven books had sold more than 200 million copies and had been translated into twenty languages. Of the top ten best-selling hardcover children's books of all time, Geisel still had two books listed in the top ten in 2001—*Green Eggs and Ham* stood in fourth place; *The Cat in the Hat* came in ninth.

Children from a Springfield, Massachusetts elementary school dressed as the famed Cat in the Hat for the installation of a sculpture of "Horton" in May of 2002.

Geisel died at the age of eighty-seven on September 24, 1991. According to those who knew him and worked with him, his influence will be felt for a long time.

"While Ted is gone, he left Dr. Seuss behind," said publisher Robert Bernstein. "As far as any of us can see ahead of us, Dr. Seuss will be around, getting young kids interested in reading, starting them and their parents thinking about the important things in this world, and giving them all a great time while doing it."[8]

Timeline

1904—Born in Springfield, Massachusetts.

1922—Attends Dartmouth College.

1925—Begins attending Lincoln College, part of Oxford University.

1927—Begins writing for *Judge* magazine. Creates Flit advertising campaign. Marries Helen Palmer.

1931—Illustrates book of children's sayings called *Boners*.

1937—Writes first children's book, *And to Think That I Saw It on Mulberry Street*.

1940—Publishes *Horton Hatches the Egg*.

1946—Receives Academy Award for best documentary feature, *Your Job in Germany*.

1947—Wins second Academy Award for best documentary feature, *Design for Death*.

1951—Receives Academy Award for the animated cartoon, *Gerald McBoing-Boing*.

1957—Publishes *The Cat in the Hat* and *How the Grinch Stole Christmas*.

1958—Becomes president of Beginner Books at Random House.

1966—*How the Grinch Stole Christmas* airs for the first time on television.

1967—Helen Geisel dies.

1968—*The Foot Book*, the first of the Bright & Early Books, is published. Remarries to Audrey Dimond.

1972—*The Lorax* airs on television.

1984—Receives Pulitzer Prize for his contributions to children's literature.

1991—Dies at the age of eighty-seven.

Books by Dr. Seuss

Books in Print

And to Think That I Saw It on Mulberry Street (1937).

Bartholomew & the Oobleck (1949).

The Butter Battle Book (1984).

Cat in the Hat (1957).

Cat in the Hat Comes Back (1958).

Cat in the Hat Songbook (1993).

The Cat's Quizzer (1993).

Daisy-Head Mayzie (1995).

Did I Ever Tell You How Lucky You Are? (1973).

Dr. Seuss's ABC (1963).

Dr. Seuss's Sleep Book (1962).

The Five Hundred Hats of Barthomew Cubbins (1938).

Foot Book (1968).

Fox in Socks (1965).

Great Day for Up! (1974).

Green Eggs and Ham (1960).

Happy Birthday to You! (1959).

Hop on Pop (1963).

Horton Hatches the Egg (1940).

Horton Hears a Who (1954).

How the Grinch Stole Christmas (1957).

Hunches in Bunches (1982).

I Am Not Going to Get Up Today! (1987).

I Can Draw It Myself: By Me, Myself, with a Little Help from My Friend Dr. Seuss (1970).

I Can Lick Thirty Tigers Today & Other Stories (1969).

I Can Read with My Eyes Shut! (1978).

I Had Trouble in Getting to Solla Sollew (1992).

If I Ran the Circus (1956).

If I Ran the Zoo (1950).

King's Stilts (1939).

Lorax (1971).

McElligot's Pool (1947).

Marvin K. Mooney, Will You Please Go Now (1972).

Mister Brown Can Moo, Can You? (1970).

My Book About Me (1969).

Oh, Say Can You Say? (1979).

Oh, the Places You'll Go! (1990).

Oh! The Thinks You Can Think! (1975).

On Beyond Zebra (1955).

One Fish, Two Fish, Red Fish, Blue Fish (1960).

Scrambled Eggs Super! (1953).

The Seven Lady Godivas (1987).

Shape of Me & Other Stuff (1973).

Sneetches & Other Stories (1969).

There's a Wocket in My Pocket! (1974).

Thidwick, the Big-Hearted Moose (1948).

Yertle the Turtle & Other Stories (1958).

You're Only Old Once! (1986).

Chapter Notes

Chapter 1. Lucky Man

1. San Diego Museum of Art, *Dr. Seuss from Then to Now: A Catalogue of the Retrospective Exhibition* (New York: Random House, 1986), pp. 23–25.

2. Robert Sullivan, "Oh, The Places He Went!" *Dartmouth Alumni Magazine*, Winter 1991, p. 27.

3. San Diego Museum of Art, *Dr. Seuss from Then to Now: A Catalogue of the Retrospective Exhibition* (New York: Random House, 1986), p. 25.

4. Ibid.

5. Judith and Neil Morgan, *Dr. Seuss & Mr. Geisel: A Biography* (New York: Random House, 1995), p. 81.

6. Thomas Fensch, *Of Sneetches and Whos and the Good Dr. Seuss: Essays on the Writings and Life of Theodor Geisel* (Jefferson, N.C.: McFarland & Company, Inc., 1997), p. 133. From Hilliard Harper, "The Private World of Dr. Seuss: A Visit to Theodor Geisel's La Jolla Mountaintop," *The Los Angeles Times Magazine*, May 25, 1986.

7. Morgan, p. 82.

8. San Diego Museum of Art, p. 31.

Chapter 2. Early Years

1. Peter Bunzel, "Dr. Seuss," *Life*, July 1989, p. 105.

2. Peter Bunzel, "The Wacky World of Dr. Seuss Delights the Child—and Adult—Readers of His Books," *Life*, April 6, 1959, p. 110.

3. San Diego Museum of Art, *Dr. Seuss from Then to Now: A Catalogue of the Retrospective Exhibition* (New York: Random House, 1986), p. 19.

4. Robert Sullivan, "The Boy Who Drew Wynnmphs," *Yankee Magazine*, Dec. 1995, p. 58.

5. Ibid.

6. Ruth K. McDonald, *Dr. Seuss* (Boston: Twayne Publishers, 1988), p. 3.

7. Sullivan, "The Boy Who Drew Wynnmphs," p. 58.

8. Jonathan Cott, *Pipers at the Gates of Dawn: The Wisdom of Children's Literature* (New York: Random House, 1981), p. 18.

Chapter 3. Starting to Write

1. Thomas Fensch, *The Man Who Was Dr. Seuss: The Life and Works of Theodor Geisel* (The Woodlands, Texas: Xlibris Corporation, 2000), p. 64.

2. Robert Sullivan, "Oh, the Places He Went!" *Dartmouth Alumni Magazine*, winter 1991, p. 25.

3. Morgan, p. 32.

4. Fensch, p. 65.

Chapter 4. European Travels

1. Thomas Fensch, *The Man Who Was Dr. Seuss: The Life and Works of Theodor Geisel* (The Woodlands, Texas: Xlibris Corporation, 2000), p. 66.

2. Judith and Neil Morgan, *Dr. Seuss & Mr. Geisel: A Biography* (New York: Random House, 1995), p. 45.

3. Dr. Seuss Biography, <http://www.infoplease.com/spot/scuss1.html>.

4. Morgan, p. 48.

5. Ibid., p. 52.

6. Fensch, p. 67.

7. Morgan, p. 54.

8. *Something About the Author*, volume 28, p. 110.

9. Robert Sullivan, "Oh, the Places He Went!" *Dartmouth Alumni Magazine*, winter 1991, p. 26.

Chapter 5. Taking Off

1. Thomas Fensch, *The Man Who Was Dr. Seuss: The Life and Works of Theodor Geisel* (The Woodlands, Texas: Xlibris Corporation, 2000), p. 51.

2. Robert Sullivan, "The Boy Who Drew Wynnmphs," *Yankee Magazine*, Dec. 1995, pp. 120–121.

3. Fensch, *The Man Who Was Dr. Seuss*, p. 56.

4. Fensch, *Of Sneetches and Whos and the Good Dr. Seuss*, p. 73. From Edward Connery Lathem, editor, "The Beginnings of Dr. Seuss: A Conversation with Theodor S. Geisel," *Dartmouth Alumni Magazine*, April 1976.

5. San Diego Museum of Art, *Dr. Seuss from Then to Now: A Catalogue of the Retrospective Exhibition* (New York: Random House, 1986), p. 24.

Chapter 6. On Mulberry Street

1. Jonathan Cott, *Pipers at the Gates of Dawn: The Wisdom of Children's Literature* (New York: Random House, 1981), p. 20.

2. Fensch, *Of Sneetches and Whos and the Good Dr. Seuss*, p. 125. From "Somebody's Got to Win" in Kids' Books: An Interview with Dr. Seuss on His Books for Children, Young and Old, *U.S. News and World Report*, April 14, 1986.

3. Ibid., p. 20.

4. Dr. Seuss, *And to Think That I Saw It on Mulberry Street* (New York: Random House, 1937), no pagination.

5. Judith and Neil Morgan, *Dr. Seuss & Mr. Geisel: A Biography* (New York: Random House, 1995), p. 84.

6. Dr. Seuss, *And to Think That I Saw It on Mulberry Street*.

7. Cott, p. 35.

8. Miles Corwin and Tom Gorman, "Dr. Seuss, Father of Yooks, Zooks and Grinches, Dies," *The Los Angeles Times*, Sept. 26, 1991, p. A1.

9. Morgan, p. 87.

10. Fensch, *Of Sneetches and Whos and the Good Dr. Seuss*, p. 96. From Warren T. Greenleaf, "How the Grinch Stole Reading: The Serious Nonsense of Dr. Seuss," *Principal*, May 1982.

Chapter 7. Wartime

1. Fensch, *Of Sneetches and Whos and the Good Dr. Seuss*, p. 80. From Judith Frutig, "Dr. Seuss's Green-Eggs-and-Ham World," *The Christian Science Monitor*, May 12, 1978.

2. Ibid.

3. Judith and Neil Morgan, *Dr. Seuss & Mr. Geisel: A Biography* (New York: Random House, 1995), p. 97.

4. *Something About the Author*, Vol. 93 (Gale Group, 1997), p. 116.

5. Fensch, *Of Sneetches and Whos and the Good Dr. Seuss*, p. 125. From U.S. News and World Report.

6. Miles Corwin and Tom Gorman, "Dr. Seuss, Father of Yooks, Zooks and Grinches, Dies," *The Los Angeles Times*, Sept. 26, 1991, p. 28.

7. Ibid.

8. *Something About the Author*, p. 110.

9. Jonathan Cott, *Pipers at the Gates of Dawn: The Wisdom of Children's Literature* (New York: Random House, 1981), p. 24.

10. Fensch, *Of Sneetches and Whos and the Good Dr. Seuss*, p. 139. From Glenn Edward Sadler, "Maurice Sendak and Dr. Seuss: A Conversation," *The Horn Book*, Sept./Oct. 1989.

11. Morgan, p. 135.

12. Ibid., p. 145.

13. Dr. Seuss, *Horton Hears a Who* (New York: Random House, 1954), no pagination.

Chapter 8. *The Cat in the Hat* Is Born

1. Fensch, *Of Sneetches and Whos and the Good Dr. Seuss*, p. 75. From Judith Frutig, "Dr. Seuss's Green-Eggs-and-Ham World," *The Christian Science Monitor*, May 12, 1978.

2. John Hersey, "Why Do Students Bog Down on the First R? A Local Committee Sheds Light on a National Problem: Reading," *Life*, May 24, 1954, p. 148.

3. Judith and Neil Morgan, *Dr. Seuss & Mr. Geisel: A Biography* (New York: Random House, 1995), p. 154.

4. Jonathan Cott, *Pipers at the Gates of Dawn: The Wisdom of Children's Literature* (New York: Random House, 1981), p. 25.

5. "Topics of the Times," *The New York Times*, January 19, 1957, p. A34.

6. *Something About the Author*, p. 116.

7. Morgan, p. 155.

8. Eric Pace, "Dr. Seuss, Modern Mother Goose, Dies at 87," *The New York Times*, Sept. 26, 1991, p. A1.

9. Dorothy Barclay, "See the Book? It Is Made with 6-Year-Old's Words," *The New York Times*, Apr. 15, 1957, p. A26.

10. Cott, p. 27.

11. Susan Mandel Glazer, Coordinator of Graduate Program in Reading and Language Arts, Founder and Director of Rider University Center for Reading and Writing, personal interview.

12. Ruth K. McDonald, *Dr. Seuss* (Boston: Twayne Publishers, 1988), p. 108 or 173.

13. Miles Corwin and Tom Gorman, "Dr. Seuss, Father of Yooks, Zooks and Grinches, Dies," *The Los Angeles Times*, Sept. 26, 1991, p. 28.

Chapter 9. More Stories

1. Judith and Neil Morgan, *Dr. Seuss & Mr. Geisel: A Biography* (New York: Random House, 1995), p. 158.

2. *Something About the Author*, Vol. 93 (Gale Group, 1997), pp. 114–116.

3. Morgan, p. 164.

4. Morgan, p. 158.

5. Edward Connery Lathem, ed., "The Beginnings of Dr. Seuss: A Conversation with Theodor S. Geisel," *Dartmouth Alumni Magazine*, April 1976, p. 26.

6. Morgan, p. 167.

7. Lewis Nichols, "Then I Doodled a Tree," *The New York Times Book Review*, Nov. 11, 1962, p. 2.

8. E. L. Buell, *The New York Times Book Review*, April 14, 1963, p. 56.

9. Morgan, p. 210.

Chapter 10. Final Days

1. Fensch, *Of Sneetches and Whos and the Good Dr. Seuss*, p. 86. From Cynthia Gorney, "Dr. Seuss at 75: Grinch, Cat in Hat, Wocket and Generations of Kids in His Pocket," *The Washington Post*, May 21, 1979.

2. *Something about the Author*, Vol. 93 (Gale Group, 1997), p. 116.

3. Diane Roback, ed., "Dr. Seuss Remembered," *Publishers Weekly*, Oct. 25, 1991, p. 32.

4. Fensch, *Of Sneetches and Whos and the Good Dr. Seuss*, p. 126–127. *From U.S. News and World Report.*

5. Gloria Goodale, *The Christian Science Monitor*, March 2, 1984, p. 2.

6. Diane Roback, editor, "Children's Book Scene," *Publishers Weekly*, Oct. 25, 1991.

7. Judith and Neil Morgan, *Dr. Seuss & Mr. Geisel: A Biography* (New York: Random House, 1995), p. 283.

8. Edward Connery Lathem, ed., "The Beginnings of Dr. Seuss: A Conversation with Theodor S. Geisel," *Dartmouth Alumni Magazine*, April 1976, p. 39.

Further Reading

Books

Levine, Stuart P. *The Importance Of Dr. Seuss* (San Diego: Lucent Books, 2001).

San Diego Museum of Art, *Dr. Seuss from Then to Now: A Catalogue of the Retrospective Exhibition* (New York: Random House, 1986).

Weidt, Maryann N. *Oh, the Places He Went: A Story about Dr. Seuss—Theodor Seuss Geisel* (Minneapolis, Minn.: Carolrhoda Books, 1995).

Woods, Mae. *Dr. Seuss* (Edina, Minn.: Abdo & Daughters, 2000).

Internet Addresses

Carol Hurst's Children's Literature Site: A brief biography with links
<http://www.carolhurst.com/authors/drseuss.html>

Early drawings of the Cat in the Hat
<http://www.afn.org/~afn15301/seussfiles/ecat.html>

Welcome to Seussville: Games, contests, Dr. Seuss events, etc.
<http://www.randomhouse.com/seussville/>

Index